20
WEST

STEVE FORD

ENJOY THE JOURNEY!

Dedicated to all the men and women across the world who design, build, fly, maintain, operate and support aviation in all its forms.

Introduction

Why write a book on aviation? Does the world need another book on flying? Probably not, and yet it is for one reason and one reason only I have decided to attempt to put into print a journey that I have been on for my entire life; not just during my working life, but since I was a child.

I have always had a strong interest in history and have always believed that as any good school teacher, politician or military commander would advocate, we learn from it. The following is based on what, in reality, has been formed from my own personal memoirs; but it also captures a time and places that in many instances no longer exists. History is, after all, what takes place today when we look back upon it tomorrow.

The reason for wanting to write this book was to provide a 'record'; to attempt, as accurately as possible, to provide a view from within the aviation industry during a period of monumental change. It spans six decades, stretching from propeller-driven transport aircraft to composite, fly-by-wire and wide-body double-decker aircraft, plucked from the pages of science fiction.

There is an old adage that if you have five pilots in a room, you are guaranteed to get at least ten opinions! To be fair, the same can be said of engineers and cabin crew . . . Therefore, I will endeavour to record events as I experienced them at the time, and allow you, the reader, to make observations and conclusions from this journey yourself.

Over the years, I have probably worked with and flown with hundreds if not thousands of pilots, and one of the biggest drivers for me wanting to write this book was not because it is about me, but because it is about them. It will also allow those who have absolutely no idea what it is like to spend a lifetime in aviation to get a sense of what it looks, feels and smells like to be embraced by such a career. It is a way of life that wraps itself around you and enters every pore as you fall within its envelope.

The aviation industry, as well as being dynamic and diverse, is a way of life, and its similarities to maritime exploits of centuries past and present cannot be ignored. It brings with it travel, exploration, emotion and, ultimately, both joy and anguish.

I will admit I have struggled with writing this book, and several times wrestled with myself as to whether I should. There is something innate in all of us to protect ourselves from harm and criticism, and I have exposed, not only myself, but the very industry I care passionately about; I have, in effect, handed it over to be "picked over" by you, the reader.

Whilst various manifestations and draft manuscripts have been pored over by family and friends, I found very quickly that it is impossible to please everyone, and whilst some wanted more technical detail, some wanted less, and where some needed more aviation history, what was covered left others cold!

The realisation, then, at the end of the process, was that all I am capable of doing is sharing the times, the people and the aircraft that I had contact with. It is therefore a 'snapshot' provided by a single individual, and not a broad overview of an entire period in aviation history. It is personal and I hope that, if nothing else, this comes through as you turn the pages.

So, take a deep breath . . . as we embark together.

Chapter 1
Snow Blind

The lights of New York City bounce off the high cloud cover and ricochet along the Hudson River to my left as we descend towards the Sparta VOR (VHF Omni-Directional Range) beacon directly in front of us.

It is late in the evening in New York on a cold and frigid night in March. New York state is still gripped by winter's grasp, having had significant snowfall earlier in the day. Ahead I can see more lights, bright and fluorescent, snaking up a ski slope. To the right of me and behind the wing stretches the Eerie Canal from Albany behind us in Upper New York state, and out to the west to Buffalo.

The clock by my right knee tells the truth: it is approaching 4 o'clock in the morning back in England and my body knows only too well it should be asleep.

The Airbus A340-600 is a long aircraft. It is what air traffic control terms a "heavy" and it is to be respected at all times, especially when operating onto contaminated runways that have patches of snow and ice. Our destination of Newark, New Jersey, is not generous in length and resides within a black hole surrounded by city lights.

I`d known before we left Heathrow what had happened earlier that day. That afternoon, after a brief nap at home in England, I had seen the news on television that an aircraft had slid off the runway at La Guardia into the perimeter fence. It was an MD-80 derivative, and pictures were being shown of it severely damaged at what appeared to be approximately 90 degrees to the original direction of landing, its nose section hanging over Flushing Bay. The news footage also showed extensive snow and ice on the ground.

The snow storm had moved on, however, and Newark had had all day to clear the runways and taxiways – although I always erred on the side of caution when it came to runway condition reports given by ATIS (airport operations broadcasts).

I tried, whenever I could, to give the first officer the choice of the handling sector on a trip; but on this occasion, knowing that an aircraft had already slid off a runway in New York that day, and the fact that the performance margins for the approach and landing into Newark that night were reduced, I elect to fly the sector. This was in no way questioning his ability, but simply acknowledging my own accountability as the captain.

I feel comfortable, warm and secure as we descend, crossing waypoints at the exact altitude, as instructed by New York air traffic control. The descent profile into Newark brings us in from the north, stepping us down in between approach and departure corridors for the myriad of other airports in the area.

We expect one of the parallel south-westerly runways and, consequently, are pulled off our heading as we approach Sparta to turn in a series of adjustments to the left onto an easterly heading, before finally being pointed in the direction of Teterboro, the whole time adjusting our speed and configuration.

We receive confirmation that the cabin is secure as we pass 5,000 feet, with the aircraft stable at 220 knots indicated airspeed. Manhattan grows in stature to my left, silhouetted against the Hudson River, the reflections stretching out towards us cut by lumps of floating ice.

We descend further and are cleared directly towards Teterboro. (The VOR beacon at Teterboro sits on the airport it serves.) Looking at the TCAS – the traffic collision avoidance system – on my navigation display, I can see other aircraft being fed into Newark. There is no sign of aircraft arriving or departing Teterboro airport.

The sense of speed can be measured now against the snow-covered landscape with black scars of buildings. Visibility is good, even though it is dark, as there is so much light from the towns and cities bouncing off the snow and ice. I can make out Newark Airport to my right, another black void in an ocean of light.

Cleared to turn right and intercept the localiser, we capture it straightaway and turn towards the runway at Newark. The glide slope captures and, with the landing gear rumbling down into its locked position, I call for the final stages of flap and disengage the autopilot. Final checks are called out and acknowledged as I settle into the rhythm of the aircraft.

I can feel the flexing of the wings as the small inputs I make are converted to control deflections using both inboard and outboard ailerons. The engines are spooled up to capture the final approach speed, and the slight drift is perceptible from the runway compared to the direction of our nose slicing through the freezing night air.

I start to narrow my senses into one thing and one thing only: the aeroplane. I know that I need to be at the exact speed on touchdown, with the right amount of rudder and aileron to remove our drift, and sufficient flare input to the elevators in order to arrest our descent without floating one foot above the runway in ground effect for the entire length of the runway. Brakes only work when the tyres are in contact with the runway.

The runway ahead has patches of snow and ice, which will resist braking effect and require full reverse thrust and anti-skid technology on each brake unit in order to slow us down sufficiently to safely exit onto a taxiway.

The last 100 feet, I find, tends to slow down, and time is distorted as everything is brought into sharp focus.

All looks normal, apart from the runway. For some bizarre reason the port authority who manage Newark Airport have de-iced the runway in lines . . . and the runway has black furrows scarring it.

We touch down, and immediately I crack the four thrust reversers into their gates and feel the spoilers killing lift from the wings and the medium autobrake pulsating as deceleration commences. I pull full reverse and we slow rapidly. I then back off from full reverse to avoid ingesting snow and ice, confident we are stopping in exactly the expected distance and, in turn, are able to take the expected taxiway exit.

Turning onto the snow-covered taxiway, we change to ground frequency on the radios and start our after landing procedures as soon as we have confirmed our taxi route; and as we trundle slowly along the parallel taxiway towards the terminal, I notice they have de-iced the surface in the same unusual way, with thinner black lines visible through the snow and ice.

Carefully turning onto the apron I follow the guidance and marshaller's signals, finally setting the brakes to Park. I look up and see the same thin black lines etched onto the jet bridge and terminal building.

Unbeknown to me at the time, I have a retinal tear in my left eye, rendering me snow blind.

Chapter 2

DNA

Where do we start?

Nothing is random, or is it? Nature or nurture? Perhaps my DNA, passed through my forefathers, had already mapped out my life.

My grandfather on my father's side, Ken Ford, had always been at sea, and returned after World War II to the cruise liners out of Southampton, serving as a steward on the *Queen Mary*. His survival of the war was put down to simply not being at sea during the conflict, coupled with not being hit by any of the bombs that fell on Southampton!

My great-grandfather on my father's side, Andrew Ford, had an even more colourful maritime history. He had been in the 7th Dragoon Guards at the turn of the century, and had a habit of going AWOL (absent without leave) and absconding. This, in turn, would usually result in him being caught and suitably punished. He finally absconded from the Dragoons on the 4th March 1905 from Canterbury, and was listed as a "deserter".

What does he do? He joins the Navy!

In those days, by the time the records caught up with you, you were well away, and the reality was the army and Navy did not really care if they pinched each other`s personnel. The trick was not to get caught.

Records show he was a leading stoker on *HMS Cochrane* based out of Sheerness, Kent, in 1907, and the records held in Kew, the public records office, show that in 1911 he was a mechanician in the Royal Navy.

In 1914, however, he left the Royal Navy and joined the Port of London Authority (PLA). He is listed as a fireman (stoker) on the *Hopper*. Everything was going very well for him, apart from the fact that war broke out and he knew he would be enlisted. So in order to keep one step ahead, he went to Portsmouth to rejoin the Royal Navy, which would have worked, except by then the Navy and army were talking to each other, the records had caught up, and he was promptly arrested as a deserter!

He ended up in Winchester prison and was given two options. Option A – spend a long time in prison. Option B – rejoin the army! So he joined the 1st Battalion Rifle Brigade, and Sergeant S/7535 Andrew William Ford spent the entire war in the trenches in and around Ypres and somehow, against all the odds, survived.

He was awarded the Distinguished Conduct Medal (DCM) which was announced in the London Gazette. The regimental history shows that the action took place on 3rd May 1915, about five miles northeast of Ypres.

The citation reads:

'Ford, Serjt. A. W. S/7535 (1st Bn). D.C.M. 14.1.16. For conspicuous gallantry. When everyone in his trench on a front of some hundred yards had been killed or wounded, except himself and an officer and two other men, and the enemy were within two hundred yards in force, Serjt. Ford and his companions by moving up and down the trench and firing rapidly bluffed the enemy into believing that the trench was strongly occupied, and they held it until retirement that night. By their bravery and intrepidity they saved a break in the line which would have prevented the safety of the subsequent withdrawal. Croix de Guerre (France) 1.5.17.' (London Gazette, 14th January 1916)

The reference to the Croix de Guerre is believed to be reference to a different engagement, where he is reputed to have saved a young French boy.

My father went to sea at the age of seventeen with the Merchant Navy. He soon concluded that this was not the future he wanted, however, and in 1955 he left the service. Knowing he would be called up for National Service, he realised that if he signed up for five years he could learn a trade and a qualification as an engine fitter. He promptly joined the Royal Air Force as a tech cert and spent the following five years in effect serving an apprenticeship. He spent time in Aden, and completed his last two years of service at RAF Swinderby, No. 8 Flying Training School, working on Goblin engines for the de Havilland Vampire.

When he left the RAF, he worked on mechanical plant equipment, before joining Farm Aviation in 1962 at Eastleigh Airport in Southampton, working on light aircraft – Piper Cubs and Austers mainly.

My father very quickly grasped the importance of qualifications and, in particular, licences after leaving the RAF, and having gained his original civil engineers' licences, he joined Management Aviation[1] in 1964 in Cambridgeshire. Management Aviation was based at Bourne Airfield, and we lived about a mile and a half around the corner at Caldecote.

His aviation career was about to take off, literally, and it was this environment I had been born into in 1960.

I clearly remember the rural location and open farmland that surrounded our cottage, the long warm summers and, of course, the freezing winters. And I

---

[1] Management Aviation maintained crop sprayers and, as well as Piper Pawnees, they also serviced and supported helicopters.

distinctly remember sitting in the cab of a Land Rover that was in our driveway. On a trailer behind it was a mobile helipad, and strapped securely to it was a Bell 47. Even then, though I knew nothing about aviation, I knew that whatever it was and whatever it did, it was cool! I was about five!

I asked my father what the story was behind that memory recently, and he recalled:

"What we used to do, in fact, was use a Land Rover and a flatbed trailer, which the pilots would literally fly onto the back of. Once it was on the trailer, we would take the rotor blades off and shove them underneath the helicopter and strap it all down. Then it would be a case of taking it all up to, for example, Downham Market in Norfolk. When the fields were soaked with rain they could not get the tractors onto the fields to spray the potato crops, so the helicopters took on the job. We would stay up there, often for a fortnight at a time."

My brother and I used to go to the village Sunday school, and on one occasion the vicar called in to check on us, at home, and asked our mother some 'innocent' questions, clearly concerned about our welfare. It transpired that when all of the children had been asked what they were having for Sunday dinner, everyone had reeled off descriptions of fine roasts and succulent meats . . . but my brother and I had said, "Bread and jam, as dad's gone off again!" The vicar, worried that we had been abandoned by my father, was relieved to hear from my mother that the reality was we had our roasts when our father was back from a trip, regardless of what day of the week it was!

My father continued to gain knowledge and experience, seizing the opportunity to obtain a ground engineer's licence for helicopters, and after a year working for Management Aviation, he joined the original Caledonian Airways that had been formed by a canny Scot, Adam Thompson. He joined to become a flight engineer on the piston engine DC-7C, a four-engine transport aeroplane built by the Douglas Aircraft Company.

I was intrigued as to what made him switch from being a ground engineer to a flight engineer at a time when, in rural Cambridgeshire, such a move would have been difficult. He told me:

"It was suggested to me by some of the pilots at Bourne. Because I was interested in certain technical problems with both fixed wing and helicopters, I would talk them into letting me go with them on air tests and observe. I was interested in the liaison between the engineering and flight side. I was conscious of the fact that you could get a defect that would manifest itself in flight, but did not manifest itself on the ground. So I thought, well hang on, if I can go fly with them, I've worked on it after all, and I can then help troubleshoot it. This was because it was always encouraged in the RAF that if you had worked on an aircraft, which I often did in Aden, they would encourage you to fly on the aeroplane. They would say 'you worked on it, you come and fly on it.' That was a good philosophy, and I never lost that approach.

"It was some of the guys, the pilots at Management Aviation, who said, 'You like to get up and do these flights, don`t you?' I told them I never had an aspiration to become a pilot, it never came into it. So they said, 'Well, why don't you become a flight engineer?' Well in those days I thought, I don`t know as that is a job with any future in it, as they might be getting rid of flight engineers. I ended up with a twenty-five-year career flying as a flight engineer!"

He then told me that the 'bible' in relation to finding work in those days was *Flight* magazine, so he used to get that and wrote away to four different companies: BUA, Trans Meridian, Eagle Aviation and Caledonian Airways. BUA ended up being taken over by Caledonian Airways (or merged as the ex-BUA employees would argue!), and Trans Meridian and Eagle both folded. The only one to come back and offer him an interview was Caledonian Airways[2]. So he went for an interview at Gatwick, and managed to

---

[2] Caledonian Airways was founded by Sir Adam Thompson and should not be confused with the Caledonian Airways in the 1990s that British Airways operated using the former assets of British Airtours. The original Caledonian Airways went on to become British Caledonian Airways (BCal), until it was taken over by British Airways in 1987 and dismantled/absorbed into BA.

get a job at the end of 1965. And that is how he got into flying, as a flight engineer. He continued:

"When I joined Caledonian I did not have a basic operator's licence for a flight engineer so I had to do the lot, a DC-7C course and an 'O' licence. What they did was they leased the aircraft from Sabena, the national airline of Belgium, so it was interesting getting a Belgian engineer talking to us and taking us through the intricacies of the DC-7C, and after three weeks take an exam!

"I was on the DC-7C for nearly a year, and then I was transferred to the Bristol Britannia, the 'Whispering Giant'. I was on the Brit for about two years, and then we got the Boeing 707-320. It was whilst on the 707 I became what in those days they called a 'check engineer' – though I preferred to call it 'training engineer'. I did not believe in the philosophy you were solely 'checking'. Some guys were 'check trappers', and my opinion was I was there as an instructor, even though I was examining their ability to ensure they were doing what they were supposed to do as a flight engineer. It worked out alright."

In 1966, my parents made Emsworth our home, as it was easier to get to Gatwick than from Cambridgeshire, and I ended up going to school in Portsmouth, catching the train daily to Fratton Station and then walking to Southsea.

I learnt the art of 'fight or flight' walking to and from school, as Portsmouth, for those of you who don't know it, does have an edge to it. Wearing shorts, a school uniform and a cap did open you up to what was technically called, 'a good beating'.

I began to read the streets, and knew when to cross or change route. Sometimes, however, you could not escape violence, and I found hitting out first would sometimes give you that split second to run like hell while your opponent picked himself up! Not something I am sure society or the police would endorse, but those of you who have grown up in big cities or naval ports will know exactly what I am talking about. It`s simply survival. Being able to read the streets certainly kept me safe over the years, especially down route.

The naval impact on the City of Portsmouth was still huge, even in the early 1970s. My grandfather, when he came back from Burma, set up a building company in North End, Portsmouth, and I believe at one time he had over fifty men working for him, rebuilding a smashed city. W. S. Powell Limited was plastered all over the Portsmouth Corporation double-decker busses, which I would sometimes jump on to avoid 'a good beating'.

From our school in Southsea we would be marched across to the swimming pool near the Guildhall, and the area in between had numerous high-rise tower blocks. This was always an interesting journey, as on occasion the skinheads, who had not been able to decapitate you with a steering wheel lock (I was actually attacked with a steering wheel lock once, but he missed, and I could run faster), had developed what, for them, was a highly entertaining sport: dropping empty milk bottles from the higher levels of the tower blocks.

In order to avoid getting hit, we would string out, so as not to form a concentrated target area. The other saving grace for us was that skinheads did not have Norden bomb aiming equipment, and also were probably not very consistent in attending maths classes. As a result, they failed to understand the importance of timing with deflection shots. On occasion, however, if we heard the tell-tale sound of a bottle 'whistling' down, accelerating towards terminal velocity, we would simply run!

I remember the city pubs being boarded up, and all of the windows having plyboard attached, both inside and outside of the windows. There was a Royal fleet review scheduled and, as well as the commonwealth fleets all being anchored off of Spit Head, the US Navy were attending, and at any one time it was estimated a thousand US sailors would be ashore. It was bizarre seeing US Navy MPs cruising the city in jeeps that they had offloaded from the ships.

The police were at Fratton, Portsmouth and Southsea, and Portsmouth Harbour train stations turning the prostitutes around and making them get back on the trains to London. They, however, were getting off at Havant, and getting taxis back into the city. I guess the city council could at least *claim* to have done their bit in attempting to 'clean things up'.

It should be clarified, however, that like all large cities all over Europe at the time, the vast majority of its inhabitants were decent people who worked hard at rebuilding their lives and communities post-war. I have a soft spot for Portsmouth and its people. It is what it is, and both it and your family roots become part of your DNA.

Chapter 3

The Original Unmins

1960-1978

Aviation is full of terminology, and 'unmins' is the abbreviated term for 'unaccompanied minors'.

My brother and I, in the 1960s, were without doubt the original unmins, as we would often be shepherded onboard aircraft and placed in the care of cabin crew, before being transferred at the other end to often another aircraft and another flight. Or, as happened in New York on one occasion, being looked after by the ground engineer's family in an apartment on Long Island. We stayed overnight, before being placed on a Pan Am Clipper jet service to Nassau in the Bahamas the next day.

Growing up, the memories I have are of travelling, constantly travelling.

Emsworth in Hampshire had now become home. This was because a year after joining Caledonian

.ys, whilst driving back to Cambridgeshire after
.1p, my father scared himself nodding off and nearly
ended up embedded in an embankment! Anyhow,
Caledonian Airways was a charter airline, and it was
not until the taking over/merger with BUA, which
was mainly a scheduled airline, that a semblance of
stability (read 'home' stability) came into the picture
whilst I was growing up.

Charter airlines were no different from
Merchant Navy steam trampers, really, picking up
cargo and passengers where they could. Caledonian
Airways would pick up troop contracts or charters
to Canada, for example, and agents would feed the
airline work, depending on where the aircraft were
at that moment in time. The work was, as a result,
extremely varied.

Rhodesia made a Unilateral Declaration of
Independence (UDI) (modern-day Zimbabwe), and
this resulted in my brother and I ending up in East
Africa, Dares Salaam, as our father was there as part of
the 'oil lift' with the Britannia aircraft.

My father recalls:

"The British government had chartered us and
we were based in Dares Salaam, flying into Lusaka and
Endola. All the seats had been stripped out and we
carried forty-five-gallon drums of either aviation fuel
or diesel. We would land and be handled by the RAF.
The government paid all of us crew £10 a trip – danger

money! – and then when we got back to England they taxed us on it, which is typical!

"The company said we could bring our family down if we wanted, and I got a message to your mother. I ended up at Southend, with an aircraft on maintenance, and you all joined me to fly back to Dares Salaam with an empty aircraft."

I remember the journey vividly, as my brother and I played football in an empty, stripped out Britannia crossing North Africa after having refuelled in Benghazi, Libya.

The two memories that stand out are, firstly, when my brother climbed to the top diving board at the hotel swimming pool and, being cheered on by an audience, dived in. The problem being, however, he could neither dive nor swim, and as he ricocheted back to the surface surrounded by bubbles, my father had to intercept him by diving in from the side. The second memory is of my mother being aghast when the current loaves being carried on the heads of woman in the market took off . . . currents having been thousands of flies!

Flying in the 1960s was still a dangerous occupation, and prior to my father joining Caledonian Airways, two DC-7s had been lost.

On 4th March1962, DC-7C G-ARUD was lost when it crashed on takeoff, with the loss of all 111 passengers and crew. The aircraft had crashed and caught fire in the jungle at the end of the runway, clipping a tree on the left bank before breaking ~~ith the majority of the wreckage on the left side of the creek (a tributary of the River Wouri).

The Flight Safety Foundation report I recently found on the internet states:

'The heavily-laden DC-7 was making a night takeoff from Douala runway 12 in conditions of high ambient temperature and humidity. After a long takeoff from the 9350 feet long runway, it gained little height. Some 2300yds from the runway end, 500yds left of the extended centreline, the left wing struck trees 72 feet above aerodrome elevation. The DC-7, named "Star of Robbie Burns", crashed into a tidal swamp and exploded on impact. The flight, a special charter flight on behalf of Trans Africa Air Coach of London, had departed Luxembourg (LUX) on March 1, 1962, arriving in Lourenço Marques (now Maputo), Mozambique on March 2. The flight left again on March 4, bound for Douala (DLA), Cameroon, Lisbon (LIS), Portugal and Luxembourg.

PROBABLE CAUSE: In spite of the very numerous expert examinations and all the tests on the ground and in flight, which the Commission of Inquiry has carried out or caused to be carried out, the state of the wreckage and its position in an inundated forest area have prevented the Commission from determining with absolute certainty the cause of the accident to DC-7C G-ARUD. The commission considers, however, that there is evidence to show that an elevator spring-tab mechanism may have jammed before impact. This jamming would have resulted in abnormal elevator control forces during the takeoff. Flight tests have shown this to be consistent with a prolonged takeoff run and a risk of losing height during flap retraction. Furthermore, the following features, all adverse, may have aggravated the circumstances in which the accident occurred: - the implementation of a procedure for gaining speed which was conducive to the aircraft being flown at a low altitude - the fact that a positive rate of climb was not maintained at the time of flap retraction which, in the SABENA procedure applied by Caledonian Airways, is not subject to any altitude limitation other than that of obstacle clearance - the presence in the co-pilot's seat of a check pilot whose attention may have been attracted more by the actions of the first pilot than by the indications on his own instrument panel. The Commission had been unable to eliminate an instrument failure as a possible cause of the accident, as the instruments were not recovered or were too seriously damaged to allow of any valid expert examination.'

(ICAO Accident Digest No.14 Volume II, Circular 71-AN/63 (36-45)

https://aviation-safety.net/database/record.php?id=19620304-0

On 28th September 1964, DC-7C G-ASID was lost when it undershot the runway at Istanbul, Turkey.

There is a report on the internet which states:

'Flight 355 took off from London for a flight to Singapore via Istanbul. The first approach to Istanbul runway 24 was abandoned because the pilot-in-command couldn't see the runway lights. Heavy rain continued as the pilot approached for the second time. VHF communications were lost during a short period of time because of a power failure in the tower transmitter and was restored when the plane was in the procedure turn. Lightning and heavy turbulence were reported during the descent and the runway was sighted when descending to 500 feet. The pilot made a slight correction to the right and ordered full flaps and power reduction to 20" boost. The plane sank quickly just short of the runway and more power was ordered, but the left main gear had struck the ground in line with the runway, 72 m short of the threshold. The plane bounced and touched down again 14 m further on. The left main gear as well as nose gear collapsed, causing the no. 1 and 2 engines to break off, followed by the entire left wing. The fuselage skidded 260 m down the runway and a fire developed.'

https://www.baaa-acro.com/operator/caledonian-airways

My brother and I were surrounded by the airline environment, and whilst we picked up on some of the stories as they occurred, it is only now that I have had the opportunity to piece together some of the events that took place. As an unmin you just assumed it was normal.

At this time, flying was not without incident, and whilst in my entire career I've never had to shut down a jet engine, my father recalls not only having to shut down a jet engine, but also a piston engine on the DC-7C. As he remembers it:

"We were over Rome and what happened was the flight engineer's position had an engine analyser on the side. You used to swing around in your seat. It was a cathode ray tube and you could actually plug into any engine, any cylinder and any spark plug.

"As an engineer's aeroplane, it was lovely, very technical. In the cruise you would have to set the engine power up by taking it to continuous boost, and then you would have to change the revs on it, and then you would alter the boost so that you would actually take it around what they called the 'detonation step'. You could increase the power without causing the detonation and maintain the smooth burning of the fuel within the cylinder. We are going back to the theory of an engine, turbocharged engines as well, because they had a turbocharger. It was a Wright engine, double row radial.

"What happened on this particular occasion was we had a change in engine noise on number 2. It was a runaway prop. It happened that on that particular aeroplane you did not have four rpm gauges you had two rpm gauges, and each one had two needles on it.

"The number 2 rpm gauge was hidden behind the number 1, and it suddenly increased away from the number 1. I had gone and checked the engine analyser, and the number 2 engine analyser was displaying just a fuzz.

"The skipper said, 'It`s number 2', and with that we shut number 2 down as it was a runaway. We were near Rome and, because we had it under control, continued. When we got on the ground, the Sabena engineer said, 'You should have left it. It would have stabilised.' We said, 'It was a runaway and we shut it down.'

"The thing is, if we had not been able to shut it down it would have been disastrous. The prop shaft could have let go and the prop come off, something that I knew had happened before to others. They actually did a three-engine ferry to get it back to Brussels to get the engine changed. But when I was back at Gatwick one day and I saw Pierre, the Sabena engineer, I said, 'Oh, by the way, what happened to that runaway prop?'

"He said, 'Oh, Norman, Norman, I meant to say . . . I am sorry. You did the correct thing, because it was the feed pipe to the piston in front of the governor and it would still be running now!' I said, 'Thank you very much.'"

With respect to the Britannia, my father recalls that all of these aeroplanes were step changes in terms of technology, and that with each technological step there would be peculiarities that would come with the aeroplane.

"The Brit was a very nice aeroplane, very good," he explained. "It was known as an electrician's nightmare, but I never had any problems with it. They would say if so-and-so did not work, just go behind the cabin door and jump up and down and it would reset.

"I don`t think I had anything shut down on it at all. You would get icing. 'B skin jets' we used to call it, because you had the propeller on the front, the intake used to take the air and it would go through 180 degrees to go back into the compressor. Then it would go back through the combustion section and thru the turbine section and then out the back. It was a free running shaft. Whispering Giant is what they called it in those days. It had Bristol engines, as well as being the Bristol Britannia. Some were ex-Canadian Pacific and some were ex-BOAC."

The introduction of jet airliners did not in itself bring with it inherent safety either, and accidents still occurred. The loss of de Havilland Comets did nothing to convince the public that the jet age was safer. But over time, aircraft, training, systems and procedures brought flying within the reach of the general public, and it was no longer limited to the rich and famous.

The aircraft that without doubt changed the transatlantic routes and had the biggest impact on long haul flying was the Boeing 707 (it had a decimating effect on the shipping industry in the 1960s). It was not, however, without its problems.

As is often the case even now, crew are often positioned as passengers to join an aircraft in another part of the world, and my father found himself doing exactly that one night out of Heathrow, with a crew on a BOAC B707 with Rolls Royce engines.

A previous incident had occurred involving a B707 with Rolls Royce engines on Monday 8th April 1968. It had taken off and a fire had broken out, with the number 2 engine falling off into a flooded gravel pit. G-ARWE landed back at Heathrow on runway 05R, but was completely destroyed in the ensuing fire.

The Flight Safety Foundation has a description of the accident, which sadly resulted in five fatalities. The source of the Flight Safety Foundation narrative is listed as being ICAO. It reads as follows:

> *'The aircraft was operating Flight BA 712 from London-Heathrow Airport to Zürich and Sydney. A check pilot was on the aircraft for the purpose of carrying out a route check on the pilot-in-command. The aircraft became*

airborne from runway 28L at 15:27 and 20 seconds later, just before the time for the noise abatement power reduction, the flight crew felt and heard a combined shock and bang. The thrust lever for the No. 2 engine "kicked" towards the closed position and at the same time the instruments showed that the engine was running down. The captain ordered the engine failure drill. Because the undercarriage was retracted, the warning horn sounded when the flight engineer fully retarded the thrust lever; the check pilot and flight-engineer simultaneously went for and pulled the horn cancel switch on the pedestal, whilst the co-pilot instinctively but in error pressed the fire bell cancel button. In front of him the flight-engineer went for the engine fire shut-off handle but he did not pull it. The check pilot then reported seeing a serious fire in the No. 2 engine. Having initially started an engine failure drill, the flight engineer changed directly to the engine fire drill. ATC originally offered the pilot-in-command a landing back on runway 28L and alerted the fire services, but after a "Mayday" call Flight 712 was offered runway 05R which was accepted as it would result in a shorter flight path.

About 1.5 minutes after the start of the fire, No. 2 engine, together with part of its pylon, became detached and fell into a water filled gravel pit. At about the time the engine fell away the undercarriage was lowered and full flap selected. The undercarriage locked down normally but the hydraulic pressure and contents were seen to fall and the flaps stopped extending at 47deg, that is 3deg short of their full range. The approach to runway 05R was made from a difficult position, the aircraft being close to the runway and having reached a height of about 3000 feet and a speed of 225 kt. There is no glide slope guidance to this runway, but the approach was well judged and touchdown was achieved approximately 400 yards beyond the threshold. The aircraft came to a stop just to the left of the runway centre line, about 1800 yards from the threshold.

After the aircraft came to rest, the flight engineer commenced the engine shut-down drill and closed the start levers. Almost simultaneously the pilot-in-command ordered fire drill on the remaining engines. Before this could be carried out there was an explosion from the port wing, which increased the intensity of the fire and blew fragments of the wing over to the starboard side of the aircraft. The pilot-in-command then ordered immediate evacuation of the flight deck. The engine fire shut-off handles were not pulled and the fuel booster pumps and main electrical supply were not switched off. There were more explosions and fuel, which was released from the port tanks, spread underneath the aircraft and greatly enlarged the area of the fire. The cabin crew had made preparations for an emergency landing and as the aircraft came to a stop opened the emergency exits and started rigging the escape chutes. The passengers commenced evacuation from the two starboard overwing exits and shortly afterwards, when the escape chutes had been inflated, from the rear starboard galley door and then the forward starboard galley door. However, because of the spread of the fire under the rear of the fuselage the escape chute at the rear galley door soon burst and, following the first explosion, the overwing escape route also became unusable. The great majority of the survivors left the aircraft via the forward galley door escape chute.

PROBABLE CAUSE: The accident resulted from an omission to close the fuel shut off valve when

No. 2 engine caught fire following the failure of its No. 5 low pressure compressor wheel. The failure of the wheel was due to fatigue.'

(ICAO Aircraft Accident Digest 18-II https://aviation-safety.net/database/record.php?id=19680408-0

A few months later the same situation happened when my father found himself positioning on a BOAC Boeing 707 out of Heathrow with a Caledonian Airways crew. He recalls:

"Low and behold, it occurred on the same side as where the engine had previously caught fire. We were in a row of three seats on the left-hand side, and there was an Indian chap sat next to me, and one of our stewardesses was also sat next to me. It was a night departure and, when we got airborne, as the gear came up, all of a sudden Bang!

"I looked out of the window and there were flames coming up over the wing, and this Indian chap said, 'Is it supposed to do that?' and I said, 'Not really, it will be okay, it's probably a fuel pipe that has gone, and if they do the procedure properly they will put it out.' I turned to the stewardess sat next to me and said, 'Are you alright?' And she said, 'Yeah, yeah, why, what's up? Have they put another light on?' and I said, 'Yeah, it's on the wing, it's on fire.'

"So, anyway, I sat there and suddenly I heard somebody scream. After we landed, because there was another crew positioning sat down the back, I said to the other flight engineer, 'I heard somebody scream?' He said, 'Yeah, it was me!' All I could think at the time was, *I hope they do the drill right!*

"When we had landed, it turned out it was the same problem as before, and eventually blade confinement programmes were introduced to prevent rupturing of fuel cells as a result of blade failures. I said to one of the stewardesses, 'Excuse me, you said when we got airborne we could have a drink?' 'Yeah, yeah,' she said, 'That's right.' So I said, 'Well, we have been airborne, so can we have a drink?' With that she broke open the champagne, and we were sat down the back drinking champagne while the firemen were outside spraying foam over the steaming engine.

"Anyway, we got off and back inside the terminal, and they gave us some vouchers to get some sandwiches. I had a pile of sandwiches and a little old lady serving said, 'Oh no, you can't have all those.' I said, 'Madam, I have just removed my backside off of an aeroplane that was on fire, and the least you could do is bend the rules slightly, please?' So she said, 'Oh, okay, go on then.'

"I phoned your mother from the terminal and she said, 'I thought you were going off to Singapore?' I said, 'Yeah, well, there's been a slight mishap, and I thought I would let you know just in case there is anything in the paper tomorrow. We were on an aeroplane that caught fire. Nobody has been hurt. They are going to wheel another aeroplane out so we are carrying on.'

"Nobody got killed, though, so it never did, as far as I am aware, make the press. The papers were not interested. We carried on and got to our destination. I think we were doing troop contracts. When we got back we had a very nice letter from Adam Thompson thanking us for continuing and carrying on."

My initial memories of the B707 are when my brother and I, after being packaged off as unmins via New York, flew on B707s, first to JFK, and then the following day to Nassau. Our parents were there, as my father had been contracted out with Caledonian Airways crews to operate a single B707 on behalf of Bahamas World.

As was often the case, it was a concoction of different resources and nationalities, and of questionable commercial viability at a time when everyone wanted to have an airline and fly their country's flag.

The aircraft was Australian and on lease to Bahamas World, the flight crews were British, the cabin crew Bahamian, and the maintenance support was provided by Braniff International out of Texas with American mechanics.

As my father remembers it:

"It was this big New York guy who managed to get hold of this aeroplane, and he was involved with Curly Walters, who procured aircraft for Caledonian Airways. Curly Walters was one of the founders as well as being an ex-flight engineer."

Routine line maintenance was carried out in Nassau, and more in depth maintenance was carried out in the hangars at Dallas, Love Field.

Memories of turquoise seas, warm sandy beaches, and being in and around B707s filled my childhood. The Braniff engineers had their families in the Bahamas as well and, as a result, when the aircraft flew up to Dallas we would all go. Not as much room inside a B707 with empty seats to play football, however, so we played with frisbees!

Family friendships developed over the years. My association with the Dallas and Fort Worth area of Texas remains to this day. I was exposed to a culture and a lifestyle that was, on the whole, unheard of in the UK, and I remember on my fifteenth birthday being in Texas receiving a Dallas Cowboys jacket as a birthday present.

Looking back, it sounds surreal, but that is exactly how it was; and anybody involved in aviation, either directly or indirectly, will know that it is not a normal lifestyle and has significant impact on the home.

Charter flying is exactly that: you are chartered, and it is both varied and time-consuming.

I remember on one occasion my father went away for what was supposed to be a few days, and a week later he came back having circumnavigated the world. He recalls:

"That was a 707. What happened was, it was a Saturday night and I was going up to do a Nairobi from Gatwick, which would get us back on the Monday. Fly down Saturday night and then, after minimum rest, fly back Sunday night and get back Monday morning.

"When I got to Gatwick to check in they said, 'Arr, we've got a problem, a 707 took off earlier to go to Los Angeles and had to turn back due to a gyro problem. We've rectified the gyro problem, but that crew has run out of hours for Los Angeles.' So, anyway, what they said was, 'We would like you to take the Los Angeles flight instead of going to Nairobi.' We said that would be okay. We did ask what would happen when we got to LA, though, and would we be bringing another one back. They told us the information would be there when we got to LA.

"We flew to Iceland, refuelled, and carried on to LA, as in those days a 707 could not do LA nonstop full of fuel and passengers. When we got to LA, the station manager said, 'You and the first officer and navigator go to the hotel. You've got about six hours.' The captain was told to position back to the UK on the aeroplane we had brought in. We asked what we were supposed to do. They said, "Well, go to the hotel and we will send transport for you. You've got to position to Anchorage, Alaska. The cabin crew and a captain will join you. An aircraft will be coming in from Toronto and you've got to take that aeroplane.' We said, 'Okay, but where do we take that?' They said, 'Hong Kong, empty.'

"We got up to Anchorage, and the aircraft arrived a day or two later. That crew positioned to LA, and we took off for Hong Kong over the Bering Sea and Japan. We arrived at ten to eight in the morning, but the airport did not open until eight, so they made us hold over Stone Cutters Island for ten minutes.

"We landed, and the following day, I will always remember, we had 187 Chinese passengers that we were taking to Bahrain. But because of the runway length at Hong Kong and the passenger load, we had to go to Bangkok first and refuel.

"About half an hour before top of descent, I lost the oil out of number 3 engine. I had the master caution come up and I said, 'The oil quantity is down and, at the moment, I don't know if it has actually gone or it is an indication?' Within a minute we got the low pressure light, which confirmed we were losing the oil and I said, 'We need to shut that engine down,' which we did, and did a three-engine landing.

"After landing there was no sign whatsoever of oil loss, and engine runs were normal with no loss. The only possible cause I could think of was loss through a breather, such as the accessory gearbox drive, but there was no sign whatsoever of that having been the cause. The problem was we had, on the ground, a serviceable aeroplane.

"What the captain and I decided was to plan on a worst case scenario of it happening again, and having a route and altitude on three engines to clear mountains en route to Bahrain. We put on sufficient fuel to cope with any possible scenario. From Bahrain, the aircraft continued with another crew, and we eventually got back to Gatwick, having been completely around the world. I subsequently found out the oil loss we had experienced had been caused by a defective number 3 bearing air/oil seal."

My father's career moved at a pace. I asked him if he felt that the airline industry was an insecure place to be in the 1960s and 1970s, with so many companies coming and going. (Something that continues to this day!)

He told me that when he first joined and was qualified, the aircraft sat around a lot. It was not until they became legitimised, per se, when they had scheduled services and did not rely just on charters, that the industry expanded. It was, however, cyclical. It still is today. Monarch, for example, have just gone under.

He explained that the reason this happens is the goal posts keep moving, and if companies don't keep up with that, they fold. Pan Am, TWA, Laker Airways, British Eagle and Cunard were, in their day, all big names. Now gone. The way to avoid this as a charter airline is go to wherever the work is. On one occasion Caledonian was chartered to position 3 Britannias to Oakland, California, to pick up ships' lubricating oil and take them to Fiji.

He then recalled how they flew from Gatwick empty to Quebec, and when they got there the temperature was so cold – it was -20 degrees centigrade – that the maxeret brake unit on the port undercarriage leaked brake fluid because the seals had gone – they had to get an air start truck to blow hot air onto it to warm it up to stop it leaking. When they got to Fiji, they thought they would be going to Honolulu to pick up cargo, but in the end went back to Oakland, and then Miami, where another charter had not materialised . . . and flew empty back to Gatwick. The company made enough money, just, from moving the ships' lubricating oil to justify the whole trip, apparently.

It was in this heady environment that my brother and I grew up. Believing it was normal.

For me the aviation industry was the very core of my world, without even realising it, and believed this was all normal; but I certainly had no aspirations of becoming a pilot or an aircraft engineer.

I was, however, interested in taking motorbikes apart, and later this developed into taking cars apart and modifying them. My brother went on to serve an apprenticeship in the motor trade, and I had a cadetship as a cadet officer lined up with the Bank Line, a shipping line with a long history of merchant trade.

It was not to be.

Chapter 4

Gunner's Runner

1978-1985

I read a book, *Supership* by Noel Mostert, that I was given by my parents as a Christmas present in 1975, aged fifteen. Suffice to say, I was going to go to sea until I read that book.

In the book, the significant changes within the shipping industry in terms of automation and flags of convenience were vividly described. From this it was obvious to me, even at fifteen, that the technological advances to the shipping industry were enormous. Ships that were adequate post-war were being quickly superseded and, as a consequence, were becoming obsolete. It was not for me.

A neighbour at Emsworth was the skipper of a coastal trader that used to sail weekly from Portsmouth to Guernsey to collect tomatoes in the summer. I would go with him and stay on the ship, more often than not getting stuck in Guernsey harbour because of storms. My memories are of vomit, peeling potatoes and everyone onboard saying, "Don't do it! Don't go to sea, you silly bugger, there's no future in it!"

So I didn't.

Instead, after school, and after a year of tearing around the countryside in West Sussex on motorbikes and in cars, I found myself standing in Hangar 3 at Gatwick Airport reporting for my first day as an engineering clerk at British Caledonian Airways[3]. It was June 1978. (I had worked in a food factory and a flour mill before writing to BCal.) By then, my parents had moved to Billingshurst so my father could be even closer to Gatwick Airport.

The airline had BAC 1-11s, both 200 and 500 series, that were maintained in Hangar 1. The hangar was at the edge of the airport on the south side next to the perimeter road and next to the railway line. In front of Hangar 1 was a large earth berm[4] that faced the runway and engineers would sit out there in the summer on their lunch break.

Moving across the apron upon which 1-11s sat, a line of hangars stretched from east to west. First was Hangar 2, which was compartmentalised into workshops. As you walked in, on your right was

---

[3] Caledonian Airways had become Caledonian/BUA, and then British Caledonian Airways Limited (BCal).

[4] A raised earth mound.

the wheel and tyre bay. In front and on your left, as you turned right on the corner ninety degrees, was the sheet metal/fabrication workshop, with various additional workshops on your right. And over the back to your left was the tech library, full of manuals and microfiche.

Hangar 2 continued west, with the corridor running along the side of the engineering stores.

It was where many an apprentice had arrived with a stores requisition for a 'long weight', and was left to stand there for hours; or a request for 'striped paint', and the storeman would pretend to phone the 'Zebra Paint Company' in Kenya.

From the corridor, through heavy rubber doors, you would push out into Hangar 3, which was enormous and a maze of grey girders and gantries. Boeing 707s, VC10s and, as they were being introduced, DC-10s and finally Boeing 747s were maintained within this vast auditorium. The DC-10's and B747's tails would stick outside, and eventually 'tail docks' were constructed.

To confuse things, Hangar 5, which consisted of the engine bay, and DC-10 hangar was next. Hangar 4 was further along and stood alone. This was motor transport. Hangar 6 was even further to the west, and was the other side of the British Airtours hangar, and only came into being when Laker Airways collapsed[5] as it had been their maintenance facility.

In front of Hangar 3 and 5 was a large ramp area, with open grass to the parallel taxiway on the south side of Gatwick`s single east-west runway. Just west of Hangar 5, at the edge of the ramp, was an engine run bay, which looked like a huge bus shelter, with girders and steel plates that would deflect the exhaust from engines under power ninety degrees up into the air. It was used for 1-11s and B707s, but not for DC-10s. Behind this was a car park.

I climbed the metal steps in Hangar 3 and, suspended on metal stilts in the air at the back of the hangar, was 'Auntie May`s' office. (May Hunt was the engineering administrator, known affectionately to everyone as Auntie May.)

Over the whole of the hangars within Hangar 3 resided the general manager, Ron Gunner. Known on the hangar floor as 'Ron Glum', due to his poker-straight face and lack of expression, he was a large man who seldom smiled.

I was later to see his more compassionate side, and he was instrumental in turning my career around

[5] This was in February 1982, and was reported by the BBC as follows: *"Pioneering budget airliner Laker Airways has collapsed owing £270 million to banks and other creditors. After a four-hour board meeting at London's Gatwick Airport, company chairman Sir Freddie Laker asked Clydesdale Bank to appoint a receiver. All 17 Laker aircraft have been ordered to return to the UK by tonight and the British Airports Authority has impounded a DC-10 at Gatwick to cover the company's landing and parking costs."*

and providing me with the opportunity to enrol in an engineering apprenticeship. And many more years later I said to a fitter, "You do know he was in a Japanese POW camp, don`t you?" "Yeah," he replied, "but we all think he was a bloody guard."

I became 'Gunner's Runner'. And I developed a huge respect for the man who, despite his stern manner, was given a warm send off when he eventually retired. People were literally lined up through the doors. He had commanded the respect of all in engineering and it was a fitting tribute.

For a year I worked my backside off. I devoured everything I was given to do as an engineering clerk and, as a result, I got to know every inch of every hangar and was in contact with every department.

I was surrounded by aeroplanes, having grown up surrounded by aeroplanes. I had staff travel privileges to spend the weekend in Tunisia or go to LA on holiday. After watching *Two-Lane Blacktop* – a film about two guys in a '55 Chevy painted in grey primer racing across America – I switched the XT500 dirt bike that I charged around on to a P6 Rover with a 3.5 litre V8, which was the closest English thing we had to a '55 Chevy.

Working in such an environment was boy-heaven and working on cars and motorbikes at home, much to my parent's angst, was the icing on the cake. Especially when they were away and I failed to rebuild a motorbike engine in time and they returned to find it spread out all over the dining-room neatly, marked out on paper plates!

Life was good.

But it was not enough, and I knew being a clerk was not going to be the career for me. What I needed was qualifications, a trade. I confided in Ron Gunner and he supported me with my application to become an engineering apprentice with BCal. Technically, I was too old, as I was nineteen when I started my apprenticeship, and apprenticeships were normally started at sixteen or seventeen. I argued, however, with Ron Gunner`s support, that the company would save money as I was already an employee, so by starting an apprenticeship I would take a pay cut!

They agreed, and on 10th September 1979 I formally became a 'technician' apprentice, specialising in airframe and engine. I knew I was a jammy bugger, as I could so easily have slipped through the net, and yet now I had a chance to focus all the testosterone and adrenaline into one thing: aeroplanes.

I was off.

For the next four years, I consumed it like I was drinking from a fire hydrant. I found that because I had worked in pubs and food factories, even a flour mill, as well as a year as Gunner's Runner, I was a bit wiser than the majority of my fellow apprentices when it came to work. A lot of them had come straight from school, and because we spent a lot of time at Crawley College to them it was just an extension of school.

It wasn't, though, and our apprenticeship was a serious one in engineering terms, as it exposed us to a huge cross section of disciplines. At Crawley College in West Sussex, next to Gatwick Airport, we learnt basic turning, shaping, fitting, electrics, milling, grinding, fabrication and electronics.

The training at college, which was a sandwich course[6], coupled with night school, enabled me to gain a Higher National Certificate in Aerospace Studies – Mechanical. In my spare time, even during my apprenticeship, I studied and obtained an FAA (American) 'A & P' licence (airframe and powerplant), which involved a lot of travelling.

I took the written exams in Frankfurt at the FAA Field Office at Rheine Main Air Force Base. The practical exams I took in the United States in hangars with designated FAA examiners. The airframe exam I took at Lubbock, Texas, and the powerplant exam at Teterboro, New Jersey.

I did not bat an eyelid at jumping on and off aeroplanes on my own, on 'standby', on my days off. It was how I had grown up. Decades later, my daughter, aged fifteen, flew on her own to Dallas Fort Worth and on to San Antonio to stay at her grandmother's ranch

---

[6] A training course with alternate periods of formal instruction and practical experience.

for the summer holidays. I had kittens! But for me it was what was necessary to achieve and gain those valuable qualifications.

It was in the early 1980s that I flew out to JFK, New York, on standby in order to grab a rental car. I drove to Teterboro in New Jersey to night stop, and then took my practical Powerplant test the following day. Being staff travel, the order of the day, certainly then, was you wore a suit and tie. You represented the company, and if you were not dressed to sit in first class, no matter where you were to sit, even if it was row 66 next to the toilet, or a jump seat in the flight deck, you were not going to get on.

On the flight over I had studied the street maps and decided that instead of coming off Long Island across Staten Island to I95 and north up to Teterboro, I would drive through Brooklyn and across the Brooklyn Bridge, across Manhattan, and through the Lincoln Tunnel. Which I proceeded to do on a very hot summer's afternoon.

As I crossed Brooklyn off the main arteries I realised very quickly I was in deep trouble. The hire car and this lily-white English boy in a suit and a tie had to be a cop, or just a stupid tourist: I was drawing a lot of attention. So I wound the radio up, slid off the tie, put on the shades, locked the doors and tried to look like I belonged there, which clearly I did not.

At each stop light, I made sure I left enough of a gap between the car in front and my front bumper, so if a brick came in through a side window, or someone got too close for comfort, I could pull out.

You have to remember that this was in the days of Starsky and Hutch, before Mayor Giuliani cleaned things up. It was a dangerous place to get lost, and skinheads in Portsmouth with steering wheel locks and dropping bottles from high rises were small fry compared to these streets.

I made it.

The next day I was sat in front of the owner and chief mechanic of the hangar facility at Teterboro, and he sat staring at me in his pinstriped suit and mirrored sunglasses. In a heavy Italian accent he said, "How was your journey?" I relayed the story of the previous day's fright, driving through areas and down streets I had no right to be on. He grinned and said, "You're a very brave young man. I only go over there for weddings and funerals . . . not so many weddings."

The hangars and workshops at Gatwick at that time in history was an exciting place to be. Boeing 707s, some passenger, some freighter, and some combi (combination freight and pax) would be scattered in front of Hangar 3, and a 1-11 would be in the engine muffler, howling with the deafening roar from a Rolls Royce Spey at full throttle.

Or an Air Malawi VC-10 would be in there, and an Air Florida DC-10 would be under tow, coming across for minor maintenance having gone 'tech' at Gatwick.

The tails of Dan-Air, Air Europe and Britannia Airways would traverse the other side of the runway in and out of the terminal area – what was then the only passenger terminal.

Gatwick in the summer was a joy, with the heady smell of jet fuel and freshly cut grass wafting across the ramp and being lifted by thermals as you sat on the embankment at lunchtime watching the aircraft come and go.

The airfield sits on a river, which is a stupid place actually to have an international airport; but it had grown from a grass runway that, in the 1930s, had an Art Deco terminal known as 'the Beehive'. Long since separated from the main concrete and asphalt runway since constructed, the Beehive is where my mother recalls flying to France in a DC-3. The Beehive is still there to this day, next to the Civil Aviation Authority headquarters on the south side of the A23. The river is now channelled under the runway. The surrounding area was originally a horse racecourse. Someone obviously thought, with it being flat, it would be a good place to operate aeroplanes from. But they were not meteorologists: low-lying flat pastures that flank a river are susceptible to fog. As a result, Gatwick is known amongst pilots as 'Fogwick'.

In addition, the hangars on the south side are exactly where south-westerly winds roll over . . . and induce low-level turbulence over the threshold as you approach the runway. After the demise of Sir Freddie Laker's airline, the turbulence which spilled off his old hangar, upsetting what otherwise would have been a smooth landing, was known as 'Laker's revenge'!

As apprentices we went into every workshop and every part of engineering to learn our craft. But, just as importantly, we learned other people's trades and limitations so we could use that knowledge later on. The hangars were referred to as the 'base', and the 'line' is the 'flight line', and is the area where aircraft are handled on turnarounds. Working with both was invaluable, but line maintenance was always intense, as the clock was ticking before the next flight out was scheduled.

We spent time on the line, and I remember the pace could be frantic in the mornings when the trans-Atlantic flights were coming in and the 1-11s were going out for the European scheduled flights, returning sometimes a couple of hours later if they had only gone, for example, across to Brussels.

The men and women of British Caledonian Airways were and will always remain close to my heart, as they were extremely professional, dedicated and focused on providing a safe operation – and this with the constant threat hanging over them of being put out of business in a volatile industry.

Anyone reading this who are ex Paramount, British Eagle, British Island Airways, Dan-air, Air Europe, British Midland Airways, Silver City, Tradewinds, Laker Airways or Monarch Airlines, will know exactly what I'm saying. And I am sure I have missed out many airlines that also no longer trade. Changing jobs in the aviation industry was once described to me as being like 'changing deckchairs on the *Titanic*'.

We can strive to be the best at what we do, but we have absolutely no control over the longevity of our employer. My father was lucky: twenty-five years were with BCal and the original Caledonian Airways; the last two years were spent on the payroll of British Airways.

We were fortunate to be trained by professionals and whilst they will probably be embarrassed for me to say so, it was the likes of Fred Ansell (the Hangar 3 foreman), Mike Self (fitter), Noel Peazold, (fitter), 'Harry the Hun' (fitter and ex-Luftwaffe), Tim Foxon (fitter), and hundreds of others who added layers to our knowledge and allowed us to grow.

Health and Safety, whilst in place, was, to be fair, reflective of the time. In other words, some of the things we did, you would not dream of doing now.

As an apprentice, and having consumed fewer doughnuts in life on account of being young, you would often find yourself inside empty fuel tanks carrying out repairs with your allocated fitter.

I remember the BAC 1-11 in particular was prone to fuel leaks, and in order to get in to add sealant or conduct a repair, the leading edges would come off and you would slide in, often with the arms and legs of your overalls just taped with masking tape to stop the fuel that was pooled on the bottom running in. Did it stop fuel burns? No. It just soaked through your overalls.

The DC-10 fuel tanks were cavernous, and because of the internal baffles and chambers you had to don breathing apparatus and have a rope around you. You were buddied up, and your 'wingman', who sat on top of the wing, was responsible for checking you were still conscious. This involved verbal abuse being shouted at you as you worked in the tank, and if you pulled on the rope, which he had in his hand, he knew you were conscious.

I remember one fitter, however, who was dragged out unconscious, having been connected to nitrogen instead of an air supply. He survived.

The years I spent serving my apprenticeship were not without incident, and sadly fitters did lose their lives at Gatwick. I recall a fitter who was inflating, I believe, a B707 wheel on the line, and the portable nitrogen bottle did not have a regulator. The result was that when he opened the bottle, which had been connected to the tyre, 3,000psi emptied into the tyre, which immediately exploded. I also remember a painter falling off of an aeroplane in a hangar – he wasn't wearing a safety harness – and suffered fatal head injuries.

Whenever we worked on systems, you always isolated the system and labelled in the cockpit 'Do Not Operate'. Unfortunately, on one occasion, the procedures were not followed correctly and, as is often the case in accidents, an 'error chain' was set in motion. The hydraulics were powered up from the cockpit whilst a fitter was in between the fin and rudder, working on the tail, causing fatal injuries.

I was witness to one particular incident that occurred on a clear day. I was walking in front of Hangar 3, which had a B707 under tow, it being pulled out at the time. I heard the roar of a BAC 1-11 taking off, and then silence as the engines were closed with what sounded like a rejected take off. This was immediately followed by the crackle of two Rolls Royce Speys at full power.

I swung around immediately, and I could not believe what I was seeing. There was one of our 1-11s, roaring into the air whilst simultaneously falling to the right, towards the control tower. It was flying purely on the fact that thrust was overcoming gravity, and for no other reason. It then swung round the control tower, heading straight towards the town of Horley. Clearly this was not a normal departure route.

I hollered at the fitters with the B707, and we all ran over to the edge of the taxiway, eyes fixated on this dot that had swung east and was currently coming around to line up with the runway. By this time, people were pouring out of hangars and running across to witness this spectacle.

The BAC 1-11 came into view, and descended towards the runway, and as it came over the railway line connecting Brighton with London it powered up again and flew a go-around. There in front of us, for all to see, was a BAC 1-11 with the nose gear ninety degrees off the aircraft centre line, pointing the wrong way. We could see the gear being retracted, and when it came around the second time and lined up with the gear down, it was locked in position, with the nose gear correctly aligned in the direction of travel.

The aircraft landed safely.

It turned out that the aircraft had been on retraction checks, troubleshooting a fault with the nose gear in Hangar 1, the BAC 1-11 hangar, at the end of which, one of the fleet pilots had been asked to do a high-speed taxi check with a couple of the engineers. Because the aircraft had been on jacks, it had ballast onboard and critically, when the high-speed taxi check took place, it was not configured for flight. As they accelerated, the aircraft pitched up and the 1-11 started auto rotating, so as soon as the nose went up the wing increased its angle of attack, generating lift, and it got airborne.

The pilot got a dressing down for not configuring the aircraft correctly, and for reaching a flying speed with an out-of-trim centre of gravity; but at the same time he was commended on his flying skills, for saving the aircraft and everyone below it, as it hurtled northwest across the airfield.

The tower was rumoured to have hit the crash button, and had started evacuating as they believed the aircraft would hit them!

It was a BAC 1-11 that nearly killed me one day when I found myself inches away from thrust reverser clamshell doors that were inadvertently deployed during an engine run.

Jet engines running on the ground are extremely dangerous. I saw a van end up on two wheels on the flight line when it was stupidly driven behind a DC-10 that was parking at the terminal. The second stupid part was, having fallen back onto all four wheels, the driver carried on driving, and the engine exhaust on the other wing hit him broadside. He did exactly the same thing, wobbling along on just two wheels, before driving off to presumably perform an emergency underpants inspection.

One day, I found myself with my allocated fitter on the engine muffler, performing an engine run after an engine change on a 1-11. It was the number 1 engine on the left-hand side, and I was crouched out on the left wing as the engine started up.

My fitter was on the headset and I was following his hand signals. The cowlings were off and, after the engine had stabilised, it was going to be my job to move out to a ninety-degree intercept of the left engine and approach it dead in the middle of the stub wing. This kept me out of the danger zones for both ingestion and exhaust. A jet engine, even at idle, can still pick a man up and suck him through like a food blender.

Once crouched underneath the engine, I was to put the back of my hand underneath the outlet of the generator cooling duct and check air was being exhausted freely, then look for obvious leaks, without moving forward or aft. If all was good, I would give my fitter the thumbs-up and move back the same way. Or, if there was a problem, run my hand in a 'cut' movement across my throat and he would order the engine to be shut down.

I was waved at by the fitter, and he simulated blowing on the back of his hand – which was the signal for me to move into position. I slid across, and I could feel the vibrations travelling through the concrete as I approached in the safe area. Crouched, ear defenders on, the vibration once I was underneath the engine and howl from the Rolls Royce Spey was intense.

I carried out the checks and swung myself, although still crouched, towards the fitter, who was also crouched and away from the nose so he could see me under the wing. I raised my thumb. As I did so, I swung my left leg out to move back the way I had come . . . and heard a whoosh and a crack as the thrust reversers, which resemble two huge clam shells, swung away from the cascade vanes and locked into the fully deployed position, just missing me.

But the engine's thrust was then directed forward, at me, and being on one leg because I had swung around, it picked me up like a rag doll and threw me towards the wing. I remember tumbling past as the whine of the engine spooled down, whilst the fitter screamed at the supervisor in the cockpit to shut it off.

It transpired that the fitter had said, "Yeah, it's all good," when I had given the thumbs-up, and the supervisor had interpreted that as meaning the external checks were complete and I was clear . . . the next step on the test schedule being thrust reverser deployment and exercising!

Thanks!

Engine runs were dangerous, and a Pratt and Whitney engine was blown up spectacularly one day on a Boeing 707 when it had been started using the air start, and was spinning as fast as it could go with fuel on and failed to light off.

The supervisor was scratching his head on the flight deck trying to work out why it would not light off and start. It was turning over, with good air from the air start. The fuel was on? He swung around and saw on the flight engineer's circuit breaker panel that the igniter's circuit breakers were still out, so he leant over and pushed them in.

Whooooomf!

Having been turning over for a long time and absolutely awash with fuel, it ignited, and the ensuing explosion in the combustion chamber resulted in the back of the engine spewing blades out of the exhaust into the engine muffler. This, in turn, deflected them ninety degrees into the air and they cascaded down on to the car park. Not good. The aircraft was duly towed back into the hangar for another engine change.

As I progressed and completed my apprenticeship, I successfully gained the CAA airframe and engine licence. I was heckled by a lot of the other apprentices for being a swot. But I didn't care. I was older than the rest of them in my intake by at least two to three years, and at that age it is a huge difference.

I do remember there were also some other swots, and we competed fiercely with every exam. Julian Day and Allan Godding were not daft. Allan, to this day, works in engineering, and occasionally, when we bump into each other, we talk about some of the antics which cannot go into print! Mainly involving Cessna 172s in Texas and 'spring break'!

In 1980 the flying bug got to me and I started flying lessons. Now I was in serious trouble! As well as working in the hangars as an apprentice, and going to college, I was taking to the skies. Flying was and still is an expensive pursuit if you are sponsoring yourself. The only way I could do it was to use staff travel and commute back and forwards to Long Beach, California, via LAX. I supplemented my meagre apprentice salary by working in a pub for a former London boxer, Sam Vandenberg. Once I had my US private pilot's license I converted it to a British one, and bought a share in a Jodel Ambassador, a low-wing four-seat tail-dragger, wood and fabric aircraft. The problem with all things aviation is it becomes addictive – not to the point that I became an 'anorak' though![7]

Technology was moving rapidly and the company, as well as taking regular delivery of the DC-10-30s, which could fly to LA nonstop, were looking at the Airbus A310, and later ordered A320s, which ended up in British Airways livery.

Avionics technology was moving very fast and the avionics apprentices were caught up with it at full speed.

Having completed my apprenticeship, I applied for and successfully moved into engineering within the 'P and D' department (project and development) as a propulsion development engineer on the General Electric CF6, which powered the DC-10s.

There I worked for Dave Jarvis, who was a boffin to put it simply, and talked in binary! But he taught me a lot about Condition Monitored Maintenance

---

[7] For non-UK readers, an 'anorak' is the term used to describe someone who stands at the end of a railway platform all day in the rain writing down train numbers . . . and wearing an anorak – or raincoat – to stay dry during the inevitable British rain!

Programmes (CMMP) and Spectrographic Oil Analysis Programmes (SOAP).

In layman's terms, we monitored every engine parameter when it flew, and looked for 'step' changes and analysed the oil for traces of specific metals. From an oil analysis, we could identify specific bearings or hardware showing abnormal wear, simply from the parts per million of different metals.

I worked closely with Bill Lamborn of GE, who was based at Gatwick. He was a straight-talking Australian, and he literally took me under his wing, bringing me along, in effect serving a second apprenticeship.

We were responsible for the engines on and off wing. This meant that in my case I would fly weekly to Glasgow on one of our 1-11s and drive across to Troon in Ayrshire and night stop. The next day I would spend at Caledonian Airmotive, the engine overhaul facility, before driving back to Glasgow and flying back to Gatwick.

In the office there was a wealth of experience, which I would lean on heavily, particularly Dave Jarvis and John Simmons. We were responsible for millions of dollars in engine budgets, so we were playing for keeps, as well as having responsibility for safety. Ian Taylor was responsible for the Pratt and Whitney JT9s, and is now CEO of Line Up Aviation, having been one of the founding directors of Vueling, the low-cost Spanish airline based in Barcelona. Mike Cotgreave looked after the Rolls Royce Speys and, being the more senior member of the team, kept us in line.

There was also Elsie, the secretary, who looked after all of us – and was actually the one who was really in charge. The departmental head (after Elsie) became Paul Chappel, who had spent the previous years at Long Beach as the company engineering representative responsible for all liaison and deliveries of the DC-10s from McDonnell Douglas.

Paul was, and remains, a larger-than-life character. Very shrewd and technically competent, he does not suffer fools. His LA suits, permed hair and mirrored glasses made him look like a 1970`s cop from Hill Street Blues! The airline industry is no different from any other, and within it there are rogues and scallywags that would cut the buttons off your shirt whilst talking to you. Paul was very good at identifying when a 'deal' was too good to be true. I learnt a lot from Paul about people, something no technical training could ever impart.

I remember years later being presented with a CF6 engine that was exactly that, too good to be true (for the price). Having been trained by Paul, I started digging and took some part numbers and, more importantly serial numbers of components. I discovered the engine had come out of a DC-10 that had crashed. It was from the number 2, middle position. The rest of the aircraft had been destroyed.

Within the aviation industry there was, and probably still is, a challenge with bogus parts. You had to tread very, *very carefully*, and make damn sure you were dealing with not only real parts but real people.

The other thing Paul did for us as young engineers was to stand behind us and support us when we needed it. This is something I experienced first-hand. When it happened I was sick to the core, believing I had screwed up and, amongst my peers, had screwed up spectacularly.

I was in the office on my own when a call came from the Operations room saying that one of our DC-10s had been in contact about severe vibration showing on the vibration N1 fan indicator for the number 1 engine. I asked if they could feel the vibration through the centre pedestal throttle quadrant, and did it move linearly with the thrust lever on the vibration indicator whenever the thrust was changed. In other words, as they increased thrust did the indication increase proportionally.

The aircraft was going to Los Angeles, but was still over the UK heading north. I pulled the monitoring sheets, and we actually had the number 1 engine on that aircraft 'on watch' due to trend analysis data. Ops confirmed that the answer to both questions was yes. They then asked, "Do you want it to turn around and come back?"

There was nobody else around, nobody to turn to. Paul was out of the office and I was the CF6 development engineer. It was obvious to me, based on the facts provided, that the answer was yes.

I grabbed the department car keys and drove down to the flight line and waited for the aircraft with the line engineers. It parked on a remote stand, with steps positioned, and passengers started to disembark onto the waiting busses.

As they were disembarking, the engineers opened the big fan cowl doors and immediately one of the hold open stays that holds the fan cowling safely open swung past their heads.

I could not believe it. I knew straightaway what the problem was, as witness marks showed clearly that the stay had been bouncing off the cowling and the side of the engine. The vibration sensor had been picking up the resonance of the engine hold open stay hitting it . . . there was nothing wrong with the engine.

One of the engineers said, "Great, looks like it came back for nothing as there is nothing wrong with the engine."

I felt sick.

I returned to the office and clearly the balloon had gone up about an idiot from the office calling an aircraft back unnecessarily.

Paul came back later, and after an hour or so he called me in and closed the door. He stood there in his pinstriped suit, wearing a waistcoat and purple shirt. He slowly lit a cigarette and said, "Look, my son, you have done nothing wrong. You did what was right based on the information you had. I have told the line that it was one of their idiots that caused that aircraft to do an inflight return because they did not stow and latch that hold open stay where it should have been. Don`t worry about it. I would rather you make a call like that and this be the result, than not have the guts to make the call and the engine blew up. Okay?"

He was right, but I still felt sick.

As the weeks, months, years and decades rolled by, this has happened time and time again. Pilots and engineers have to make decisions based on what they are presented with. On every single occasion I was in that position, I was backed up, for which I am eternally grateful.

Paul, along with Roy Gardner and Dick Plowes, went on to establish Virgin Atlantic Engineering in the early days of Sir Richard Branson's fledgling airline. I distinctly remember walking through Hangar 3 one day seeing Virgin's one and only aircraft having an engine change prior to its inaugural flight the next day. The year was 1984. Little did I know the future would hold seven years in the left-hand seat of the 747 for me, three years on the Classic -100/-200, and four years on the -400.

Engineering is where it was at and, in many ways, still is. Over the years, even during my flying career, I continued to have an active interest in and maintain an affinity with my engineering roots. It certainly opened doors and presented me with career opportunities I would not otherwise have experienced.

The engineers I worked with were highly skilled and competent. We had our own workshops, covering various disciplines from engines, sheet metal fabrication, brake and wheel overhauls to cabin seats and interiors. The apprenticeship training encompassed all of these disciplines, with time spent in each workshop. The work itself would often be varied, therefore, and ranged from the routine scheduled maintenance tasks to heavy maintenance. I found myself replacing complete belly skins on 1-11s and, on other occasions, working on DC-10 pylon modifications, all as part of a team of engineers.

There were two main camps on the hangar floor: airframe/engine and avionics engineers. The avionics engineers were responsible for the radios and navigation equipment, so generally were not exposed to hydraulic fluid burning their skin, or the tightness around the stomach as you were lowered into a fuel tank. We were referred to as the 'grubbers', and the avionics engineers were referred to as the 'fairies' – completely politically incorrect, but that is the way we saw it in those days!

The hangars were referred to as the 'base', and the flight line across the other side of the runway as the 'line', as previously explained. Some people gravitated to the line, preferring the excitement of interacting with the aircraft and the crews, whilst others preferred the hangar environment and the slim hope of an early 'trap' – getting out early before the end of a shift!

Both environments have moments and their fair share of dangers.

Working on the line during a pushback is, and remains to this day, a dangerous place to be. With a headset and face-cup mask you are literally tied to the aircraft, walking beside the nose wheel as the tractor unit pushes what can be 350 tonnes of aluminium and fuel off the gate.

Beside you is a tow bar connecting the tractor unit to the nose gear. If it shears it will whip around and take your legs off in a second. So you always, always, position yourself to one side, clear of the potential arc. If the headset itself becomes entangled with the nose wheel it can pull you under and turn you into pulp. Add the jet engines to the equation – which can pick a man up from fifty feet and suck him through and slice him to pieces – and you might reasonably begin to question your career choice.

'Safety, safety, safety' was the mantra, and for a damn good reason.

The Boeing 707s were being phased out and we had a fleet of DC-10s, BAC 1-11s and a B747. The only VC-10 we ever saw was an Air Malawi aircraft. Rumours were that we were getting A310s from Airbus, though.

When Laker Airways folded, Rank Leisure asked BCal if they would help out with looking after two DC-10-10s that were ex-Laker aircraft, in order to complete leisure market customers' requirements for their own brand. It was a huge success, and with ex-Laker crews it seemed like a sensible idea to continue with what started as BCal Charter, then named Cal-Air, and eventually branded Novair. I was to become deeply involved in the operation, initially looking after their engines.

Looking back on it all now it was exciting working at 'Fogwick' for BCal, and a bit of a roller coaster; and being Gunner's Runner had resulted in total aviation immersion and, at the end of it, I was a qualified aircraft engineer.

But it was not enough. I wanted more. So, in June 1985, I left to pursue a professional flying career.

Chapter 5

Self-improver

1980-1987

As an apprentice I was in what can only be described as 'sponge mode' in that I would absorb and soak up any knowledge that came my way. It therefore naturally followed that I would gravitate to Shoreham and Goodwood, the two local airfields, at the weekend.

In 1980 the flying bug got to me and I started flying lessons, initially with Toon Ghose Aviation. Toon, an Indian pilot who was a character to say the least, is remembered fondly by all who flew at Shoreham in the Seventies and Eighties. He always finished off the day in the Art Deco terminal building at Shoreham with a brandy and milk. Toon sadly passed away in 2019.

It was on the 9th February 1980 at 1105 in the morning that I had my first lesson at . . . Goodwood. Why? Because it rains a lot in England, and Shoreham was flooded (and in those days there was no paved runway at Shoreham and it was all grass).

Toon had moved his aircraft over to Goodwood, and even though it too was a grass airfield, it was not as flooded as Shoreham! Toon's aeroplane was parked outside of Vectair flying club. I was introduced to Ed Luckett, my flying instructor, and I was off on exercises 1 to 4. Two weeks later the aircraft were back at Shoreham (Cessna 152s), and I continued my training.

It was expensive – boy was it expensive! – and I paid for it all myself from my apprentice wages and by working in the evenings at the Five Oaks Inn, a pub north of Billingshurst on the A29, where the road forks to Horsham. (Long since gone, the only thing left being the pub sign on what is now an auto dealership.) The landlord, Sam Vandenberg, was an ex-boxer from the east end of London. He looked like he had been hit by a double-decker bus; but, most importantly, he was a big fella and very capable of making sure I did not get 'a good beating' when I worked there.

The pub had a saloon bar with an entrance on the Horsham side (the posh side), and a public bar with an entrance on the A29 side heading north to Dorking (the rural side). Sam and his wife Olive would tend to manage the saloon bar, and I would be on my own in the public bar. Every so often he would stick his head in and say, "Are they giving you any bovver? If they do, just let me know." Then he would shout out, "Alright, lads, you lot bloody behave!"

The pennies earned would be poured into Toon`s milk and brandy fund and, by May, with twelve hours five minutes under my belt I was let loose and flew my first solo: a red entry in my log book to identify such a significant event!

However, as anybody who has trained in the UK will testify, the weather is the biggest factor and it slows you right down, especially if you are working full time, as I was. You could easily go a month of wet weekends, and when you did finally fly, all you were doing was re-capping what you did five weeks earlier to blow off the rust. In training you need continuity, you need to attack it focused on what it is you are trying to achieve and, with flying, you need good weather!

By October of that year I was sat there with eighteen hours and five minutes in my log book, having progressed only six hours since May. This was clearly not going to work. So I decided to take full advantage of the fact that I worked for an airline and fly to where the training was a) cheaper, and b) where the weather was virtually guaranteed to get you in the air, often twice or three times in the same day.

So on 5th January 1981, I found myself in a Cessna 150 with an instructor taking off in the late afternoon from Long Beach, California, to Compton, Los Angeles. Returning to Long Beach, I'd conducted stalls, area familiarisation, airport familiarisation and a practice forced landing. I flew seven times in four days. This was more like it!

It was a no brainer to pour my time and money into gaining my licence in the States, and I settled into a Winnebago that was parked on the driveway of the resident BCal engineer based at McDonnell, Douglas. We would drive from Garden Grove along the 405 freeway, and I would be dropped at Eagle Aviation. I still remember coming off the freeway by Signal Hill to the airport, clear blue skies and the radio playing, 'Once in a lifetime' by Talking Heads.

BCal were still taking delivery of DC-10s, and Long Beach was a massive airport in a completely different league to Shoreham and Goodwood; but it never ceased to amaze me (and amuse me later on in life) when people would sneer at those of us who went to the States or Canada to train and gain licences and experience, always citing that an environment of big open airspace and blue skies could not possibly provide the level of experience you could get in the UK watching the rain lash against the window on a flooded airfield!

The reality was far different, and something those who had not experienced it would never understand.

Long Beach had five runways providing ten landing configurations: two parallel north-south, two parallel east-west, and runway 12/30 at over 10,000 feet long, cutting across the lot. You had an FAA control tower with ground frequencies, heavy jet traffic, with DC-9s and DC-10s, business jets, helicopters, and training all on the same airfield.

Sea mist was prone to roll in and fog out parts of the LA basin. There was mountain flying and associated turbulence. There were dozens of similar airports surrounding it and, of course, LAX, with a complex layer-cake of airspace. Throw in the U.S. Marine Corp, Navy and Air Force, and it made for what is commonly known as 'shark-infested custard'! Over the top of LAX was (and still remains) a VFR corridor for aircraft that students like me would transit across. Try doing that at Heathrow!

The first thing I learnt, however, with flying, and particularly light aircraft-flying in the States, was that nobody made it a big deal. The country is so vast that transport and communication links are vital to connect thousands of square miles of wilderness with towns and cities. Most states had an 'Aeronautics Commission' that would ensure towns over a certain population had a municipal airport. Infrastructure would be put in place, and T-hangars, fuel, ramp areas, and sometimes mini terminal buildings. All with no landing fees applied. It was federally supported, with a partnership approach that ensured it was uniform across the country.

In those first four days of flying in Long Beach, before flying back home, I also flew to Chino and

Hemet Ryan. Chino is a war-bird mecca, with Planes of Fame and numerous other museums on site. Seeing P-51s taxiing around, and Corsairs from the US Pacific Fleet in World War II, was not unusual.

My instructor, and someone I will always consider as a friend, was Joe Santoro. Joe was of Italian descent, but had a manner and calmness that was anything but Italian. I never saw Joe flustered and, boy, did I give him reason to be on occasions. He was always cool, calm and collected which, as any student will testify, is critical.

In April of 1981, I used my leave and was back at Long Beach. Flying from the 10th to the 24th, I flew thirty-four trips, the last flight being my FAA check ride with Colleen who, upon passing me as a 'private pilot', said, "Always remember that this is a licence to learn. Never forget that."

She was right. If there is one thing that you never ever stop doing, it is learning. Flying is a very humbling experience; if you think you know it all, it is time to stop.

The next month, having converted my licence to a British one, I was checked out at Goodwood near Chichester by Doug Adams in one of his two Cessna 150s. Vectair and Goodwood was cheaper than Shoreham, and is a beautiful setting, nestled against the South Downs (which has since then become a National Park). It was closer to the Isle of Wight, too, and offered plenty of areas to explore, including Hayling Island, Portsmouth Harbour and the Solent.

My very first passenger was my girlfriend. The flight lasted for exactly fifteen minutes. My log book entry reads: 'Passenger window opened on take-off. 1 circuit and returned.' As I got airborne she knocked the window latch with her elbow, which popped up due to a worn pin and swung out into the airstream. The prop wash promptly threw it against the underside of the high wing Cessna. She was screaming. I was shouting over the noise to reach out and pull it closed, which no way in hell was she ever going to do for fear of the door popping open – after all the window had flown open! – so I had no choice but to continue the circuit and land.

Doug from Vectair had watched the whole thing and thought it was hilarious. Vectair was a flying club which operated out of a brick storeroom between the Ladies' and Gents' rooms on the airfield, run by Doug and his wife 'Scotty'. Doug was a Brummie and had been a Mosquito pilot in World War II. Having been pulled out of a Blenheim after crash landing, he was in hospital when he took a shine to the nurse that looked after him: Scotty.

My girlfriend was not amused; but, to give her credit, three days later we flew to Selsey Bill, along the coast to Arundel Castle and back to Bognor Regis, before returning, without incident. Colleen had been right: this was a licence to learn.

I was checked out on a Cessna 172, and started to gain experience. I flew as much as I could out of Goodwood, but it was always the cost that limited the flying. There was no getting around that fact that you could fly two to three hours in the States for one hour in the UK. And all I wanted to do was fly, so I started using all of my leave and spare time to make trips out to the States and hire aircraft for what became my own Magical Mystery Tours: I would convince fellow apprentices to join me and, sharing the cost of the hire, we would go off on adventures.

I found a small municipal airport out in the northwest Texas panhandle called Slaton, which is just southeast of Lubbock (of Buddy Holly fame). Slaton municipal was run by Vietnam War veterans who organised the different branches: helicopter, fixed wing training, and crop dusting.

They had an old trailer on the airfield that we could use, and an old land boat of a car that we called 'the Limo', which could, according to the band the B52s, hold about twenty! The Limo would be our chariot of choice at night to go to The Circle, a country and western club on the edge of Lubbock.

Marshall King flew the Pawnee crop duster, and Colonel H Robert Hall, who must have been in his sixties at the time, was an ex-B52 pilot. Bob Beeze was an ex-Cessna Bird Dog pilot, and must have been six foot four at least.

It was interesting flying, as being ex-Vietnam pilots, Marshall and Bob certainly had a completely different 'fear' threshold from the rest of us. I remember watching Marshall spraying a field one evening, when the wind had dropped and he was running the length of the field to the end where there was a line of power cables. He would fly under the power line, pull up in a tear drop, arc using the rudder to turn at the apex, and dive back down under the same cables to level off, feet above the crop, and start spraying again! I have a photograph of him flying the Pawnee that evening, silhouetted against the setting sun . . . an iconic image etched in my mind forever.

Marshall was also prone to wreaking havoc on the highway that ran from Post, Snyder and Slaton up to Lubbock. After spraying, back at Slaton he would fill the hopper with water and go off to blow water through the spray nozzles to clear them out, this being necessary in order to clear out residual chemical. (I remember the airport and even our trailer reeked of chemical!) Having cleared out the nozzles he would then have to dump the water out of the hopper, pulling what was nicknamed 'the money handle'.

The money handle was an emergency release valve that if you were spraying a field and had, for example, an engine failure, you could pull and dump your chemical load: lose the weight, convert speed into height, and try to land off of it, obviously without a hopper full of chemical in front of you. Marshall thought it was highly amusing to hunt for solitary cars on the highway after the spray nozzles had been cleared, especially convertibles. Approaching from behind, high enough not to be heard or seen, he would pull the money handle . . . and dump a microburst of rain from an invisible thunderstorm onto the unsuspecting car.

One day he took it a step too far, however, as at the end of Slaton`s valley was a canyon that had recently claimed the life of a government marksman and Super Cub pilot. In a Super Cub, the marksman had been in the back as part of the coyote cull that took place to keep numbers under control and protect live stock. The pilot was so fixated on following the coyote, that when it darted into a crevice in the side of the canyon, the pilot instinctively followed it into the canyon wall.

We could hear the roar of the Pawnee in the canyon, and out leapt the underside of the aircraft from the far end of the airfield above us. We all saw the grey cloud of water spewing out as Marshall pulled the money handle; but we watched in horror as this column of water smashed into our beloved trailer, causing carnage.

The flying was superb, though, and it opened up the whole of Texas to me. In a Cessna 172 we would go off for days and explore. I would only ever take two friends from the hangars at Gatwick with me on those trips, as a 172 with four onboard in the Texas heat simply did not work, especially with the density altitude around Lubbock (the Cap Rock of the Texas panhandle was over 3,000 feet above sea level).

But we covered vast distances, often down to Fort Worth, where I had a lot of family friends from my childhood when my father had been flying for Bahamas World. We would then continue on down to the Texas Hill Country, and then on to Harlingen in the very southern tip of the state. We would also fly to Corpus Christi on the Gulf Coast, and all points in between.

Some of the flights were at the maximum endurance for the aircraft, and also my bladder. One flight, from Robstown down in southeast Texas near Corpus Christi to Snyder in the panhandle, is listed as three hours twenty-four minutes in my log book. An entry next to it reads: 'Filled an orange juice bottle […] 435 nautical miles.' I remember asking – I think it was Allan Godding – to fly straight and level (which he had probably not done before) whilst I slid my seat back and filled the bottle that was to become my life saver. As any pilot will tell you, there is nothing worse than bursting for the restroom on an approach and you start to feel your legs shake! On this occasion, problem solved.

In 1984 I flew mainly out of the Houston area, from David Wayne Hooks Memorial Airfield. In addition, I flew more out of the UK, as I had bought a share in a Jodel Ambassador DR100A.

The Jodel was a big four-seat, solid aircraft; but being wood and fabric with a tail wheel, it was, in my humble opinion, really only any good with two people onboard. In France the aircraft had been used to fly newspapers around, and you will find people who love them; but I always thought it was under-powered and it did not inspire me with confidence.

The aircraft was kept at Redhill Aerodrome, in the Tiger Club hangar, and the Civil Aviation Authority gave me dispensation to use my CAA airframe and engine licences to carry out 100-hour inspections on it.

I never truly enjoyed flying from Redhill. The airfield was squashed against the Gatwick control zone, and with London Heathrow to the northwest was limited in terms of open air space. You invariably flew east out towards the county of Kent. As a result, I continued to fly whenever I could from Goodwood. And when I was at Prestwick, working with Caledonian Airmotive in the summer, and fulfilling my role as a propulsion development engineer, I would also fly a Grumman Cheetah along the coast from the local flying club, making the most of the long evenings.

I flew as an observer in my capacity as a propulsion development engineer on a DC-10, and was in the flight deck on the jump seat behind the captain. We flew for two hours fifteen minutes, and I had a box of electronics on the floor measuring vibrations from various engine sensors. My log book entry simply says, 'TEST FLIGHT. 4 circuits. Autoland CAT 3A certification, vibration analysis. Not logged as operational crewmember.'

But it was still not enough, and I realised I wanted to try and get a commercial licence and fly professionally. It was the above flight, in G-BEBM, that had made me realise this. It was 8th November 1984.

I knew what I had to do.

I sold everything. Aeroplane share, cars, motorbikes. I worked extra shifts at the pub, and ploughed towards the summer of 1985 intent on resigning from BCal and going out to the States to build more hours and gain my licences.

When I resigned, everyone thought I was nuts. "What on earth are you doing?" they asked. I was twenty-five. I had a good well paid job in an exciting industry working for a first-class airline, and I was being told by my peers that I was mad!

For me, though, it was just logical. I could not satisfy this insatiable urge to fly aeroplanes, and I countered everything said to me with, "Well, if it does not work out and I end up back here on the hangar floor with my toolbox at my feet, I don`t care. At least I will have tried. If I don't try, I will spend the rest of my life wondering, what if?"

From the summer of 1985 to the summer of 1987 I was back and forward to Texas. I was flying as much as I could. I was fortunate that family friends put me up initially, and it meant I could concentrate on gaining first my commercial licence, then my instrument rating, followed by an instructor's licence, and eventually, years later, an airline transport pilot's licence both in the States and in the UK, separately through Air Atlantique at Coventry.

I used to stay in a trailer on Bourland Field, just southwest of Fort Worth, with a dog called Floyd, a Colt .38 under the bed, and access to a Chevy pickup truck. (I did not want the .38 but was told it went with the trailer!)

Dick Bourland was a captain with American Airlines. He looked exactly how an airline captain was supposed to look in the eyes of Hollywood: handsome and dashing. But he was also very astute commercially, and imparted a lot of that knowledge on me, the 'limey pilot'.

I ended up hour-building on a variety of aircraft and with the help of Bo Reed and Sony Page, two local real estate businessmen who kept their aircraft on the airfield. I flew Beech Barons and Cessna 182s – two completely different types of aircraft.

The C182, more often than not, I flew into strips on ranches, clearing the livestock off and buzzing the ranch foreman's trailer to get him to run the pickup out to meet us. Whenever Bo and Sony went on hunting trips, I was always included, and whether it was deer season in Ozona or Quail in Beeville, the 182 high wing Cessna, with its 260hp engine, got us in and out – not without its issues, however, as it was well known that if you flew the approach too fast it would porpoise in the flare, and, if you were not on top of it, crunch the nose and crease the firewall (something fortunately I was able to avoid).

Another American Airlines pilot, Bob Satterwhite, had a Cessna 182 too, and let me fly it for 'fuel', which was an extremely generous offer and one for which I will forever be grateful. He taught me how to fly the aircraft accurately, and if there is an aircraft to this day I have a soft spot for, it has to be the Cessna 182.

The Beech Baron I flew mainly was a -55 model with a Colemill conversion. What this meant was that two 300hp engines were bolted on in place of the original 260hp engines, and it was a rocket ship. The good news was it could haul the weight out of hot and high strips with a bit more get up and go. Density altitude, a condition that in effect thins the air for aerodynamic lift and engine power, is a killer if not understood and catered for when calculating take-off and landing performance. Having extra engine power helped.

The downside, however, was that on one engine in the Colemill-powered Baron (or any twin for that matter) you had to be on top of it and not let it go below the 'blue line' minimum controllable airspeed. If you did, you would run out of directional control authority. In other words, you were going to crash and not walk away.

We went all over the States with that aircraft, and we even took it to the Reno Air Races in Nevada via Las Vegas. Sony gave me a cup of quarters and said, "Shoo-shoo, go have some fun, limey."

We left Vegas in the late afternoon, as temperatures started to drop, and landed after sunset in Reno. The next morning I pulled back the curtains, having executed an instrument approach the previous evening in the dark, and said "Wow" when I saw the hills, mountains and cumulogranite. It was one thing to see them as numbers on a chart; quite another to stare at them in the cold light of day.

One day, Bo and Sony asked me to put my engineering hat on and jump on a 'paraffin chicken' – their name for a Boeing 737 – and fly up to Chicago in order to look at a bank-repossessed -58 model Baron. "What do you want me to do up there?" I asked. "Goddammit, if you like it buy it!" was Sony's reply.

So off I went, and what I found was a stretched Baron (being the -58 version) with double doors on the right-hand side opening up to the club seating. The first thing I did, which I always did, was sit down and read the log books. I wasn't interested in looking at the aeroplane; I was always interested in the log books. That is what tells the story. New paint, new interior?

Not interested. The maintenance history, however, I am very interested in.

And there it was. Bingo! Clear for all to see written in the engine log books. The advertised 1500-hour engined -58 Baron had had a brand new factory engine six months earlier, installed on the left-hand side, forty hours since new. (The bank did not know they had an aircraft with a higher than advertised value.)

Towards the end of the day I gave the aircraft a thorough initial inspection, and completed the inspection the next day. After taking Sony's advice, I made a low ball offer, and after arguing over a couple of hundred dollars I bought the aeroplane (with Sony's money!) That aircraft ended up in Mena Arkansas getting paint and a new interior, before they sold it on.

During this time, I managed to get some right-hand seat time in a King Air C90, courtesy of Sony's extended family who appeared to own Lufkin, a small town southeast of Dallas; but things were changing rapidly in the UK, and the yuppie generation were in control. It was time to return permanently.

In May 1987 I returned to the UK, and this time stayed. I was immediately contacted by Bill Lamborn, the General Electric engine company rep at Gatwick who I had worked with previously. Laker Airways had folded and British Caledonian had been approached to operate DC-10-10s for the summer season by Rank Leisure. This was to cover their holiday market.

The aircraft had been repainted in the colours of British Caledonian Charter, initially to separate the operation from the scheduled services of BCal. Pilots and management were ex-Laker. The flight operations director was Vic Smith, who was very similar in character to Ron Gunner, and could certainly be intimidating. But he, too, turned out to be a gentle giant. When we met and he told me what he wanted me to do, I was neither intimidated nor swayed from my focus on becoming a commercial airline pilot. The aircraft had suffered some engine challenges that needed to be addressed and sorted quickly, and I was happy to help out, but only on a part-time basis so I could concentrate on flying.

Almost immediately, on the 11th June, I found myself in the cockpit of G-GCAL, flying to Alicante taking engine performance data. My log book reads: 'Not logged as operational crewmember, Engine 45115 installed. N1, N2, FF, EGT data. OATL calculated. Engine Number 3.'

I could not have timed my return better. Everywhere I looked there was work! I took my British exams, and at Coventry I did the British instrument rating in a Cessna 310 (twin) at Air Atlantique.

If ever you need a job you have to get off your backside and get out there. Sending a CV and waiting just does not cut it.

If you are hungry enough, you will find food, and I was now ready to embark on the next chapter as a commercial pilot, and it was time to start knocking on doors.

Chapter 6

Junior Birdman

1987-1990

At Biggin Hill[8] in the spring of 1988 I knocked on the right door. Surewings was a small charter operator flying all over Europe and I timed it just right, without knowing, as it was the very day their co-pilot had resigned to join Air Europe. They operated a Beech King Air 350 for a carpet company and also used it for ad hoc charters. My little bit of King Air time in Texas was a big help opening that hangar door. (Our hangar had a red Hawker Hunter outside, and it was poignant as Keith, the chief pilot of Surewings, was an ex-Hunter pilot.)

That was a Friday. On the following Monday I was greeted with, "We want you to study for a different

---

[8] Biggin Hill is a very famous Battle of Britain fighter station that took a hammering in the early years of World War II Everywhere you look you can see its provenance; from the perimeter concrete around the edge to blast pens, and even a Spitfire as a gate guardian. History envelops you.

aeroplane and get type-rated." I remember feeling a little let down, convinced it would be a piston twin like the Baron or a Cessna 310. But no, it was the Cessna Citation . . . a jet! They hadn't mentioned on the Friday that they also operated on their Air Operators Certificate 2 Citations, which they flew not only to Europe but also to the Middle East. I was away: jet time, jet experience and challenging flying!

It was exactly a year since I had returned from Texas and in that year, whilst maintaining the health of the engines for BCal charter that had since become Cal Air, I had gained a UK commercial pilot`s licence and instrument rating. On the 25th May 1988 I flew as co-pilot in one of the Citations on a positioning flight from Biggin Hill to London Heathrow. I logged thirty minutes of jet time as we were vectored all over the South of England to slot in with the arrival traffic. Time to spare? Travel by air!

Ad hoc charter was always exciting, as you never knew where you were going to end up or for how long. It was an environment I knew only too well, having seen my father head off not knowing when he would return! The flights took me all over Europe from Paris Le Bourget to Greece and Eilat on the edge of the Red Sea (Gulf of Aqaba) in Israel. Passengers varied from businessmen to honeymoon couples and wealthy individuals who simply wanted to avoid the airlines.

The flying was demanding, and it required another level of precision that honed your skills, and not just in the physical flying but also the pre-flight planning and decision making. Within an hour of being told where you were going you could find yourself doing everything, from the pre-flight planning to official travel coordinator, from arranging taxis to booking hotels. The airports themselves would often be off the main airline networks and required a lot of negotiating with handling companies and refuellers, as well as dealing with customs and immigration requirements.

As a junior birdman and co-pilot you did a lot of the running around; but the rewards were spectacular.

One trip in August took us from Biggin Hill to Oslo in Norway. From Oslo we flew on to Torp to the south, and then to Germany and Sylt, which is an island in the Frisian archipelago in the North Sea. From Sylt we continued on to Nice in the South of France, having flown four sectors in the same day.

After four days in Nice we flew to St Moritz in Switzerland, and landed at Samedan, from where we continued, after lunch, back to Biggin Hill with our passengers. Samedan is at 5,600 feet above sea level in the Swiss Alps, surrounded by mountains. The trick with visual approaches into the airport was getting as close to the side of the valley as possible, and I remember being continually told "Get closer!" as I made my first visual approach. "If you don`t get closer you will smack into the mountain the other side when you turn!" Keith would point out.

What this sort of flying taught me very quickly was how to manage energy and, most importantly, the radius of turn due to speed. In simple terms, if you are doing 250 knots and make a 180-degree turn you will swing out a lot further than if you were doing 160 knots. Think of it as a tennis ball on a piece of string that you spin around your head. The tennis ball is going a lot faster the further out it is from you! So you would configure with partial flaps and get the aircraft to a position where you had plenty of stall margin at thirty degrees of bank, but at the same time have the lower speed where your radius of turn would not cause you a problem.

I also flew a lot with Terry Braganza, who was completely different from Keith in both his character and approach to flying. Terry had a relaxed, genteel nature; Keith would cajole on occasions, which was not always conducive to a positive learning environment. But Keith toughened me up to the standards required and, being ex-Air Force, did not accept failure as an option.

The aviation industry in the United Kingdom was going through significant changes at this time. Air Europe had shaken things up with what was to prove to be a disastrous attempt at challenging the national airlines on short-haul dominance. It was not until the true low-cost carriers entered the market did real change take place, however.

Lord King was running British Airways and his approach to competition was ruthless. British Caledonian Airways Limited (BCal) had always been a thorn in the side of British Airways and BA got what it wanted: control of BCal. It was presented as a merger, but the reality was it was a takeover and the airline was swallowed literally overnight.

Politics, as always, played a significant part in events and what was British Airtours, the leisure arm of British Airways, became Caledonian Airways, operating L-10-11 TriStars with the Golden Lion livery.

British Airways by default now owned a share of Cal-Air International, but Rank Leisure called foul and bought them out, with rumoured option clauses retained by BA. Cal-Air International was rebranded eventually as NovAir International – not to be confused with Novair in Sweden which formed in 1997 – the rumour being that someone senior in the Rank organization was driving down the M1 following a Vauxhall Nova and said, "That will do!"

My father was fifty-three at the time, and when the BBC announced the following, he was convinced his world was about to collapse:

'1987: Great British airline ready for take off
The two biggest airlines in the UK are to merge and create a carrier to compete with America's giant Air corporations. One time rivals British Caledonian (BCal) and British Airways (BA) have agreed a deal worth £237m.'
http://news.bbc.co.uk/onthisday/hi/dates/stories/july/16/newsid_2503000/2503947.stm

My father did not know it, but he was to end up benefitting from the takeover.

BA had a compulsory retirement policy for aircrew (as did most airlines then) of fifty-five and, as a result, my father found himself flying for a further two years for BA, wearing their uniform and flying the same DC-10-30s in BA livery before being retired on a final index-linked pension scheme. Looking back, he readily admits that it was the best thing that could possibly have happened for him personally. These days, retiring at fifty-five on final salary pension schemes, certainly in the airline industry, is not an option.

This was all going on around me and I knew I had to keep moving forward with my flying career. I flew every chance I could for Surewings, and rapidly built up time and experience on the Citations which, in turn, secured me two interviews and simulator assessments with Dan-Air and Novair.

The Novair opportunity came about because, in addition to working for them part time as their propulsion development engineer, I picked up on the fact they were placing orders for two brand-new Boeing 737-400s. As soon as I found out, I was straight in Vic Smith's office with my CV! There are two things Vic did that I will always be grateful for, and one was tell me straight that just because I worked for them it did not mean it was a shoe-in. I had to pass the assessments and interviews. But the second thing he did was give me a chance to prove myself: it was up to me.

I flew the Boeing 727-100 simulator as part of my assessment with Dan-Air, and the DC-10-10 simulator with Novair, ten days apart. By the end of the year I had two job offers: one with Dan-Air and the other with Novair.

I joined Novair International.

In January 1989, I found myself on my way to Seattle via Vancouver with Robin Cox, John Karman, Mac Rahman and Roy Byway to start a manufacturer's type-rating course. Seattle in January is bleak; in fact most of the year it rarely shows itself as being anything other than the UK on a grey day. Industrial and gritty, we arrived with bitter snow and ice driving across the Puget Sound.

We also arrived in Seattle to the news that a British Midland B737-400 had just slammed into the embankment on the M1 whilst on approach to East Midlands Airport near Kegworth, with tragic loss of life and serious injuries.

I was paired up with Robin Cox. 'Commander Cox' was ex-Royal Navy and had flown Buccaneers off of *HMS Ark Royal*. Robin would later go on to be the chief pilot at Virgin Atlantic and, to this day, still flies, currently operating a private Global Express for a private client. Robin could not have proven to be a better mentor. Crisp and guttural with his use of the Queen's English, he could just as easily have been at home sailing with Drake into the teeth of the Spanish Armada. Above all else he was disciplined and, coupled with my engineering building block approach, we worked well together, safely navigating our way through the intensity of a manufacturer's course.

On April Fool's Day, 1989, I found myself at Shannon trying to push the runway back into the North Atlantic, base training – endless touch and goes, flying the real thing rather than a simulator. On the 6th April I rode jump seat as Robin flew his first line training sector. The airline was desperately trying to train us all in preparation to fly the upcoming holiday season and, as a result, had us flying line training sectors all over the UK and Northern France. Wherever there were cheap landing fees, we would descend out of the sky like vultures.

In late April, with John Karman as captain, we were signed off on our final line check and released to fly revenue services. The summer schedule for the two Boeing 737s had them based in Glasgow and Manchester where, due to the aircraft's relatively long range, we could reach the Canary Islands and Greece. European destinations included Geneva, Palma, Tenerife South, Iraklion, Milan, Alicante, Athens and Ibiza, to name but a few.

Being charter configuration, with no first class or bulkheads to break up the cabin, it was like looking into a cinema auditorium. The aircraft could hold 170 passengers, which for a B737 was a lot. (But rumour had it Dan-Air had managed to get 172 into theirs!)

The company kept us in hotels, both in Glasgow or Manchester, and for blocks of six days at a time they would be our bases of operation. You would start on earlies, then migrate through late afternoon flights and finish on nights. By the end of it you were exhausted. Two days off and then you had to do it all again. I remember coming off a radar approach into Manchester in the early hours of the morning, enveloped in mist and rain onto the ILS, and realising that the weather was exactly the same as when we had departed twelve hours earlier the previous evening!

Carrying my 'licence to learn' in my flight bag I gained valuable experience, not just in flying but dealing with all the vagaries of the airline environment.

In Glasgow we lost five passengers before we even pushed back one night, as they had been dragged away to the cells by Strathclyde police officers! We were delayed, and the airline handling company had issued £5 light meal and refreshment vouchers to the passengers. As a result, 170 Glaswegians had potential access to £850 worth of McEwans beer and the ensuing brawl resulted in police intervention.

One afternoon, in Reus, Spain, we were sat facing the runway, lined up on the ramp with Britannia Airways Boeing 737s. We were waiting for the busses to ferry the passengers out to us and were quietly doing the paperwork, heads down. I looked up and saw two Canadair water bombers in bright yellow, with red stripes, join downwind and trail in line towards the coast, before turning in towards the runway in front of us. I watched in awe as the first one came in hot and high, diving towards the runway, which he was clearly going to touch down on halfway along. (Not a big problem for a turboprop with shorter landing distance requirements!) The big yellow amphibian water bomber, with its landing gear hanging down like the arms of a chimpanzee, impacted the runway, shearing off the right-hand gear. Sparks and dust flew up as the aircraft slewed to the right, pointing directly towards us as it abruptly came to a halt.

"Bloody hell!" I exclaimed.

Turning towards me, oblivious of what had just happened, the captain (who had been filling in the tech log) said, "What?"

"He`s just crashed!" I said.

As if in slow motion the dust cleared, and I could see the other aircraft had landed on the threshold and stopped, without running into the disabled aircraft in front of him. Eventually a single fire engine sped across the ramp and taxiway in front of us and headed over to the broken aeroplane, looking forlorn like a seagull with a broken wing.

"What`s going on?" called one of the crew, who was stood in the gangway behind us.

Turning around and leaning over the back of his seat, the captain said, "Bloody idiot`s only gone and crashed on the only runway. They are all right, but they're not going to shift that in a hurry."

Within minutes one of the Britannia captains came bounding up our stairs at the front and popped his head in with a, "Hello, chaps, bloody inconvenient, but we have a plan!"

Britannia Airways were a charter operator like us, but were not only far more established at the time but also had a bigger fleet and a lot of experience.

Heavily delayed on a Greek Island one hot afternoon I had been extremely impressed by the 'stiff upper lip' and 'Goddamnit, we are British, so let`s make the best of the situation and enjoy ourselves', attitude of Britannia crews.

Bed change day, when hotels accepted new tourists, tended to be a different day of the week at different resorts and countries. For example, Alicante was Friday, Palma was Saturday, and Tenerife was Sunday etc. The tour operators managed it that way so all the aeroplanes would descend on the airport the same day. Bus companies knew that one day a week was the airport runs, and the rest of the week was tours.

The only problem with this was when you had the Brits streaming across the channel, and LTU and Condor heading south out of Germany with the Scandinavians hot on their heels, and the air traffic system would grind to a halt due to lack of radar coverage and procedural (ten-minute) separations. In the height of the summer season, especially in Greece, it would bring the whole schedule down.

So I was extremely impressed when, having all been given two- to four-hour departure delays by the Greek air traffic controllers, the Britannia crew parked next to us decided to have an afternoon tea party. They duly opened their over wing exits and spread blankets on the inboard section of the wing, and the girls started hoisting up their skirts, leaning against the fuselage or sitting on the wing catching some rays, whilst tea and cake was passed out of a bar cart jammed in the aisle by the exit! And the captain was sat on the very end of the wing with his legs over the edge, swinging them back and forward eating an apple, just as he would do on the pier at Brighton.

I pointed this out to our cabin crew, thinking it was a marvellous idea. Our crew, who were all from Glasgow, laughed and said, "Look at us hens, laddie! Do you think we would last five minutes out there with all of these freckles! It's why God made us ginger so we wouldn't be stupid enough to go outside!"

Anyway, back to Reus! The Britannia captain shared his plan with us as if it was perfectly normal for aircraft to crash on the only runway, saying, "I have spoken to our Ops chaps, and they said the parallel taxiway is wide enough and the same length as the runway, so they are speaking to the tower about opening it up as a runway so we can depart."

And that is exactly what happened.

Whilst nobody landed on it, the taxiway was authorised to be used as a departure runway and, with approval from our own company, we and all of the other aircraft took it in turn to backtrack and, using full power, take off for home. I remember, however, as we started our takeoff roll, seeing tumbleweed rolling across in front of us, and thinking, *This is not a good time to suck one of those into one of the engines. They* were huge; the size of a golf cart!

Thunderstorms were always a constant threat, especially over the former Yugoslavia heading down to

Greece, and seeing St. Elmo's fire[9] on the windscreen, blue tentacles of static was a common sight. You always avoided thunderstorms by flying upwind by as large a margin as possible; but sometimes it was all around you, and the overhangs or anvils would stretch for fifty or more miles. (Ice build-up would be measured simply by the amount of ice visible on the windscreen wiper blades!)

On calm clear nights you had to be extremely careful of visual cues deceiving you. It was a strange phenomenon, but at night, approaching a runway on an island when the sea was calm and there was not a ripple of turbulence, it could appear as if the runway was twice as long as it actually was.

I saw this first-hand one night, when it looked like we were high and going to touch down halfway down the runway when, in fact, we were correctly aiming for the threshold. The runway lights were reflecting off the surface of the sea, and stretched out visually in front of the shoreline – traps for the unwary. Fortunately I was with a captain who had seen it before and pointed it out to me straight away.

As summer plunged into winter (autumn did not appear to exist in Glasgow or Manchester), the company looked at more and more exotic destinations

---

[9] A weather phenomenon in which luminous plasma is created by a corona discharge from a sharp or pointed object in a strong electric field in the atmosphere (such as those generated by thunderstorms or created by a volcanic eruption).

for our customers and decided upon India, which sounds good, but the B737-400 is a narrow body single-aisle charter-configured aircraft and is slow (by jet standards).

However, we soon found ourselves flying trips to Goa and Trivandrum in southern India, which was fast becoming 'the place to go' that season. The aircraft would fly to Rhodes, then on to Sharjah in the Middle East, where another crew would continue to Goa and then onto Trivandrum, before operating the reverse.

A lot of the passengers were originally from India, and there would often be language challenges, both on the ground and in the air. At Goa, I remember a cabin crewmember could be heard telling an agent, "You look very smart, sir!" and, "I do like what you are wearing." Confused, we asked what was going on, and she said he had been asking for compliments. Tactfully we tried to point out that what he meant was he wanted 'complimentary' freebies – tins of soda and pens etc!

On another occasion, on the way back, a crewmember came onto the flight deck all in a huff and said, "They are bloody rude some of them."

"Why is that?" we asked.

"They have no respect for women at all. One of them keeps insisting his wife is a 'vegetable', saying 'My wife is a vegetable' over and over again. Bloody rude."

Trying to hide the tears streaming down our cheeks, the captain managed to clarify that what he had been trying to say with his poor command of the English language was: My wife is a vegetarian!

Novair was a very small company and the pilots I flew with were, on the whole, extremely experienced, sharing knowledge and pointing out pitfalls, or simply suggesting a different tact when they could. It was a challenging flying environment, and everyone had to work together as a team.

Most charter airlines use the winter to plan for the next summer season and, during winter, heavy maintenance and training also takes place. I could not believe my luck when I was chosen to move onto the DC-10 in February 1990. It was the dream ticket! I had just turned thirty, and I was going to fly the DC-10, an aircraft I had been associated with for the previous decade as an engineer.

Type-rating courses are intense. Different manufacturers have different systems and equipment to learn. The aircraft itself has to be handled differently, and what you can do in a Boeing 737, for example, in terms of energy management, would not work in a big heavy wide body such as the DC-10. But the training was superb, and we were prepared well for flying what would be an exciting network, varied in that it mixed European destinations, like Alicante on bed change day, with Orlando in Florida via Gandor, Maine. (The DC-10-10 did not have the range or centre fuel tank and centre landing gear of the long range DC-10-30).

In February and March of 1990, I completed the written exams and simulator training ready to go base training with the aircraft and complete the 1179, with which I could submit to the CAA an application for a type-rating onto my licence.

The bombshell that fell was devastating: the Rank organisation decided to shut down the airline and cease operations on 31st March 1990. There was supposedly a lack of interest in acquiring the airline, and we could not help but feel politics was at play, which nobody at the time could prove, especially since the operation had reputedly been profitable.

In one fell swoop, the only other operator in the UK with wide body capacity at the time in the charter market, other than BA owned Caledonian Airways, was wiped off the aviation map. The airline could easily have cancelled our course and put us on 'garden leave'; but, to give them credit, they didn't. Mack Rahman and I completed our course, and on the 20th March 1990, ten days before the airline ceased trading, we flew to Shannon.

My log book reads: 'G-BJZE Gatwick to Shannon, initial line sector, ILS 24, Missed Approach Procedure, ILS Touch and Go, VASIS off, Touch and Go, Raw Data (2) Full Stop, Captain Geoff Andreasen.'

We spent the night at Shannon, whilst the others on the course completed their base training. Then, on the 21st March, I flew a further forty-five minutes in the circuit on two engines (instead of three) with Captain Chris Radford.

With my 1179 completed, I was straight down to the CAA when we returned and stamped in my licence was DC-10!

With two hours and forty-five minutes total time on the DC-10, now what would I do?

Chapter 7

To Err is Human

How long is it since man first flexed a flimsy piece of fabric with sufficient forward motion to provide separation from the earth at Kitty Hawk?

How long is it since open exposed cockpits gave way to aluminium and glass? And converted bombers flew the wealthy and adventurous across the English Channel to sip champagne on the Champs Elyse?

Pressurized capsules resembling automatic bank mailing tubes with wings transport humanity, with no discrimination of race, colour or creed, into the future to the east, and into the past to the west.

The jet engine, with its ability to compress distances to the journey time of a commuter train, propel us across the planet with no regard for its size, whilst we run a finger down a menu produced on paper resembling papyrus, trying to decide between the lamb and the salmon (gone are the days of just chicken or beef).

A cabin crewmember (no longer stewardesses or stewards) provide refreshments to replace lost fluids in the dehydrating atmosphere; video screens provide entertainment in whatever form we choose.

It's sad that air travel has lost much of its original glamour; it has not, however, lost its challenges. The world has not changed because we have a choice of drink and films onboard. The rain squalls that sweep across the runway at New York's JFK do not abate because we are sat in business class with our credit card and telephone, talking to a loved one on the beach in Santa Monica.

The outside environment does not yield to our attempts to control it.

The ice will stick; it will build up and change the shape of the wing; it will weigh down the aircraft, making it work harder. Ice will peel off in the slipstream around the engine intake, and some will bounce off the leading edge of the wing. Some will find its way into the engine, smashing into a fan blade, striking it like a tuning fork, the resonance reverberating throughout its entire length.

This is what ice will do. This is what ice has always done.

The dangers are there, as they were for Bleriot and as they were for Lindbergh. It is man's adaptation and human endeavour to develop the necessary technology that allows us to move around this planet with such ease.

Very rarely as we travel in the twenty-first century do we get it wrong: the person at the controls, the person designing the aircraft, closing the rear baggage hold, computing the weight and balance for flight, or controlling its progress through space, they each perform their role from a highly trained seat.

But when we do get it wrong . . .

The Dallas Fort Worth Airport (DFW) sits in the middle of a prairie in between two cities. To the east lies Dallas, with its skyscrapers clustered around its heart; the heart which stopped beating the day President John F. Kennedy drove through its arteries. Sophisticated with its wealth, and strong in its desire to place itself on the map, Dallas moves to its own beat day and night.

Fort Worth is where it is said the west begins, with its vast rail yards and stock yards. It has always traded off the land, be it through thousands of heads of cattle or barrels of oil. Fort Worth is a working town.

It was 2nd August 1985, and a hot sultry Texan day. It was no different to any other summer's day, and it was often pointed out that west of Fort Worth in the summer even the rattle snakes carried water canteens. Blue sky, heat shimmering off the roofs of cars, distorting vision, making a tree look contorted and fluid as if made from rubber. The insides of cars are capable of burning any exposed flesh that dares to slide across its surface. Cracks grow longer on the ground, rupturing it like a loaf twisted apart.

The lakes around Dallas and Fort Worth are vast, with fingers pursuing the course of ancient creeks and rivers. The odd dead tree fossilised into position, juts out from the surface as if an ancient Excalibur. The lakes draw those who are free from work to their banks.

I flew three times that day. Flying from the southwest of Fort Worth, I crossed the city and looked down on the marshalling yards and sinuous streets radiating from downtown. Flying over Carswell Air Force base, I could make out the giant plant of General Dynamics, within which F-16 fighters were being assembled. B-52 bombers, at that time the free world's mainstay for nuclear deterrence, stuck to the concrete as if born of a Jurassic age. KC-135s, derived from the Boeing 707, flew circuits below me, engine exhaust drifting in the wind.

The blue, later in the day, gave way to white as the first cotton buds expanded into fair weather cumulus; not high, but three to four thousand feet over the lakes, prairie and concrete of Carswell. The pattern was established, as it was most days, with heat and moisture providing the energy for the formation of a thunderstorm.

Mid-afternoon is when they usually appear. Sometimes as a solitary air mass storm developing in isolation; sometimes as a line, as if forming a portcullis for the unwary. From the Red River that divides Texas and Oklahoma, they stretch out to the southwest, linking with other thunderstorms over the lakes and down to the hill country in central Texas. If associated with a frontal system, they would hide, out of sight and out of mind, not prompting judgement as they loiter amongst grey veils of cloud; but they are not hidden from radar, with its all-seeing, all-knowing eyes, stabbing into the storm, stripping it of its secretive veil.

An L-10-11 TriStar approaching DFW International airport had radar, as did the Boeing 727s, DC-10s and other airport users that afternoon. The flight service station on the ground tracking weather and storm cells used its radar, too.

The thunder storms were around, forming over the lakes and forming over the land, not static but in motion, moving up and down internally, transporting columns of air with the thermal energy, lifting them higher and higher. From the top they were boiling and bubbling like cauliflower heads, vaporous folds rotating as they climbed. In the centre, rain would fall from the core due to the condensation taking place at altitude, changing the potential energy of the air mass and causing lightning. Continually moving in three dimensions, tracking east towards the suburbs, towards the shopping malls they spread out, crossing road junctions with their sheets of rain spray-painting the roads silver, closing in on the cities as though they were legionnaires marching forward.

The airport in its path is ignorant of its power.

The known was catered for as everyone knew not to fly into the core and vectored around, avoiding the core, avoiding the lightning and avoiding the shearing plates of steel rain within.

The unknown waited, waited. Neither prejudiced nor judgemental, the columns pushed down from the base of the storm, shearing across the surface of the earth, changing the direction of the wind, changing the rules of aerodynamics in its path.

The big trijet was well established on the ILS. The exchange, as recorded by the cockpit voice recorder and published by the NTSB, picked up on the pilot commenting that the rain felt good as they approached the threshold of the runway. What they did not know was that they were about to experience a micro-burst that would push the aircraft into the ground . . . short of the runway.

The first impact was the main landing gear tearing across the highway, slicing into cars and killing a motorist. As the aircraft was wrenched across the threshold, it hit a water tank and wreckage was thrown across the concrete-embalmed prairie of the airport.

I flew around the north side of DFW, clearly seeing the storm but oblivious to the tragedy that was unfolding out of view. I landed some twenty minutes later and, having put the aircraft away, went to the trailer, grabbing a soft drink from the fridge, flicking on the TV. And then I saw it.

I sat in shock, realizing it was the storm I had watched grow all day, from nothing, from a blue sky.

I still, to this day, recall the advice that I was given by an old bush pilot all those years earlier whilst flying in Texas: "Son, there are three things that kill young aviators: the weather, the weather and the weather.

The only thing I would add to that is: you don't have to be young.

Chapter 8

The Dragon's Breath

The howl was intense: the sound of a tornado approaching from behind, or was it a subway train, forcing the air in front as it sped towards the platform?

We were stretching against the shoulder harnesses, scanning the engine instruments, both independently analysing the information, both absorbing the meaning of indicator positions, the low flicker of cathode ray tubes reflecting off the cockpit windows.

The aeroplane was hanging there, nose up and howling in distress as the engines drew in air, violently compressing and igniting it with jet fuel to provide the thrust to keep us there, hanging, pointing towards the heavens. Time was standing still, as were we; suspended in time, outside looking in. There was no motion. It was as if the simulator was frozen, as if the instructor had leaned across and turned off the motion.

But the altimeter was telling the truth: we were at 33,000 feet with nothing but clear air between us and the sea below, the map display showing a magenta highway in the sky, stretched out on the screen in front of us.

As night enveloped us, I could not see up, down or either side. I was digesting, consuming, assessing and computing; poring over the myriad data we were presented with since the upset.

How long had it been since then? Since the unexpected encounter with air tearing across itself, broiling and turbulent, grabbing at the Boeing 737, as if in disgust at its utter contempt for the forces of nature?

How long had it been since we had asked the controller for a route to avoid the distant storms?

"386 request."

"386 go ahead."

"386 request direct Demos due weather."

"Roger, 386 cleared direct Demos, report Demos."

There it was, Demos in the distance, a point in space, a waypoint upon which to focus. Entering the waypoint into the navigation computer I had pressed Enter and we banked towards the north. The Canary Islands were ever further behind us as we stretched out over the Atlantic, West Africa to our right. It had looked fine: the thunderstorm cells being painted by the radar were from fifty to 300 miles away. Scattered and easily circumnavigated, their centres glowed on the screens like ripe apples pulsating as the radar repainted them with every sweep, green claws reaching out towards us, cutting our path as the magenta line upon which we flew guided our journey through the night.

We had been independently tilting the radar and had built up a picture of the storm cells as they beat their rhythmic tune upon the Atlantic. The green vapour portrayed on the screens radiated from the storms, depicting possible jolts and jars, similar to driving over cobblestones.

"Belt them in," said the captain.

Without replying I switched on the seatbelt sign.

The captain commanded a lower Mach from the auto throttles, slowing us down to the turbulence penetration speed.

The stars were intermittently visible, halfway down the windscreens, and then darkness enveloped our world. We were in and out of the tops, too heavy to climb with passengers and fuel for the long slog north.

We sat there in silence, secure in the knowledge that we had taken all the necessary precautions, and that in half an hour, with the storm behind us, we could accelerate back up to our cruise speed and cut through the night towards Edinburgh.

The captain had been sitting there with his left hand rubbing the stubble on his chin. It was close to midnight, with five more hours before we would be bussed from Edinburgh back to our hotel in Glasgow. His fingers twisted the end of his moustache, not full, but as worn by RAF pilots in World War II as a mark that, yes, they were pilots. The captain's, however, showed his Russian ancestry and it broke the Slavic breadth of his face.

It was there over the Atlantic in late October that, entrusted with 170 Scottish vacationers, we were prodded. Not just prodded but poked. Not poked but thrashed, as we touched the first wave of the dragon's breath. The stars that had been fleetingly visible disappeared as my neck whipped back and the aircraft plunged over the abyss. Or was it over? Or was it through? The wings curved up to clap hands as if in a final applause. The engines on either side of the Boeing flexed sideways, swinging their mass in disgust at the abuse. The throttles slid forward to maintain the commanded speed. My eyes rolled up, obscuring vision as they moved inside my upper lids, the weight of my skull forcing down with my shoulders and upper torso, pressing me into my seat. The aircraft remained as a mass in constant motion, travelling through the air horizontally whilst pivoting about its centre. The cobblestones were boulders jarring my knees; the sound that of metal clapping and galley equipment bouncing on stainless steel.

Stop.

A howl. A roar.

No motion, no vibration.

This wasn't the real world; the real world didn't sound like this.

The engines! It must be the compressors stalling, trying frantically to draw air in but unable to due to the expulsion of its innards from the front.

No.

N1, N2, fuel flow . . . vital signs, pulse normal.

How long were we hanging there, clawing at the night?

"Speed!" the captain shouted.

The autopilot was unable to follow the magenta line to Demos; unable to do anything but hold our wings level, but level to what? Our nose was high and there it was, the awful truth: speed . . . lack of speed, for the aircraft was nibbling at the edge of flight, holding onto altitude as was asked of it in blind obedience . . . but at a price, trading off speed, washing off speed, back now to a low level, getting slower.

"I have control."

The captain disengaged the autopilot and pushed forward, simultaneously squeezing the sides of the throttles, releasing the clutch on the auto throttle. Pushing the throttles forward to max cruise power, we descended, banking towards Porto Santo to our left, accelerating.

I informed air traffic of our descent and, as we reached a safe speed and as our confidence returned, we levelled off at 28,000 feet, five thousand feet lower.

Still surrounded by the dragon's breath we continued at 28,000 feet. Nothing appeared to be wrong with the aircraft and it flew as it was designed; and passengers and crew were unscathed, ignorant of the drama that had unfolded in front of the bulkhead separating us. Re-cleared to stay at 28,000 feet, we waited until we were lighter and then climbed gingerly back up to 33,000 feet – and found ourselves in the clear, enveloped in a canopy of constellations. I tilted the radar up and down: the nearest visible storm was forty miles away. The radio hummed as aircraft called to check we were alright, having heard the discussions with the air traffic controller, eager to avoid a similar encounter.

But we were naïve.

Naïve for thinking that we had suppressed, subdued and conquered the elements.

Chapter 9

Ah, de Havilland

1990-1993

As soon as the shock of being given thirty days' notice had sunk in, due to the sudden shutting down of the airline, I immediately started firing my CV off, applying to everyone I could think of, as did every single unemployed pilot from Novair[10].

I had a call fairly quickly from African Safari Airlines on a Friday, asking if I could get to Holland on the Monday to take a Dutch Air Law examination and join them operating a single DC-10 from Europe to Africa on charters.

I politely declined.

After a couple of weeks I received a call from a gentleman called John Horscroft, who said we

---

[10] A lot of the other ex-Novair pilots were scattered far and wide, but some joined a small scheduled airline founded by Richard Branson: Virgin Atlantic. Others were with a restructured British Island Airways (BIA), Dan-Air and Air Europe.

had flown together years earlier when I worked for Surewings. He recalled, and I remembered clearly, how I had been at Biggin Hill one afternoon and was asked to drive down to Gatwick and fly with a captain who had to conduct a certificate of airworthiness air test on a Citation business jet.

The Citation was based at Gatwick and belonged to a small operator. It was due its annual flight test where, in accordance with the flight test schedule, performance is checked.

I had met John, who was tall, well-spoken and an absolute gentleman. He had wavy hair and had been wearing a jacket and tie, as if he was about to present a country estate to a perspective purchaser. We had got on well, and with my mechanical brick-by-brick engineering background, I had acted as a flight test observer, filling in the reams of paperwork as he put the aircraft through its paces over East Anglia.

Now, years later, he proceeded to explain to me on the phone that he was actually a test pilot for British Aerospace, and my CV had landed on his desk at Hatfield, where he worked. Would I like to pop up? he wondered.

Within days I met John at Hatfield[11], on the north side of London in Hertfordshire, and I remember

---

[11] Hatfield had been founded by Sir Geoffrey de Havilland, having moved his operation from Stag Lane in London due to the increasing encroachment of the city. His logic had been that by being far to the north, the city would never grow to reach him. The late Sir Geoffrey was to be proven wrong, as I was to find out.

driving through the airfield gates into what I can only describe as a film set. It looked like the war had just finished, with row upon row of military-style buildings and Nissen huts, leading towards rows of hangars facing the runway. The security guards wore 1940`s MP-style uniforms with peaked hats and clipboards tucked under their arms.

The aircraft that sat around were up to date, however, with Bae 146s, a high wing four-engine regional jet, and 125 corporate jets, some with drab 1960`s paint schemes and others wearing loud bright colours. Two worlds had clearly collided.

On the 15th May, after sitting my written exams, I started flying with John in G-TSAM, an HS125-800B, having been employed by British Aerospace Commercial Jets.

It was a period of instability, not only within the aviation industry but personally, too, as a fledgling pilot in a viscous commercial environment could be cast aside at any time, and often was. This was not aimed at pilots personally, but was the nature, and still is, the lot of being a pilot; but all a pilot wants to do is fly.

What I desperately craved and needed at that point in time was stability, and it made perfect sense to me that British Aerospace would be able to provide that; after all, they were a manufacturer and people wanted aeroplanes. More importantly, they would, or certainly should, continue to want aeroplanes.

My ability to combine engineering and flying was not lost on me, and British Aerospace is where I wanted to be; but it was a marked change to go from heavy airliners back to business jets, and the 125-800 series in particular was very, very light on the controls. So much so I did not find it that rewarding or pleasurable to fly at first. I did over time grow to like it, however.

What the -800 made up for in light handling was in performance and comfort, offering very good mid-sized cabin space for the passengers and tremendous versatility in terms of where it could operate into and out of. As a result, it was a huge success in the United States, and the majority of the aircraft were exported there.

For me British Aerospace was the right choice at the right time. I had always got a lot of pleasure, and still do to this day, from the engineering side of aviation; it was the mechanics and technical side that I grew up with, and the ability to combine that interest with flying, which, don't get me wrong, I equally enjoyed, pulled it all together. Working for an aircraft manufacturer that was developing new products was a great way of combining the two.

Bae[12] at the time, as well as developing variants of the 146 were also developing the Bae 125-1000, which was a 125 on steroids with a new Pratt & Whitney

[12] Bae was an amalgamation of a number of British manufacturers, and consisted of what was previously Hawker, British Aircraft Corporation, Vickers, Scottish Aviation, Avro, de Havilland and numerous others.

powerplant. I thought the identity of Bae would be set in stone, but I soon found out that all of the sites and factories hung on to their former identity, and a 'silo' mentality was prevalent . . . and never did the twain meet.

The first time I landed at Woodford, just outside of Manchester, I was asked by the engineer who chocked the aircraft where we had flown in from. When I said Hatfield, he just raised his head and condescendingly said, "Ah, de Havilland," and walked off.

Welcome to Woodford!

I found myself on my own as I had flown in with Graham Bridges, the Hatfield chief pilot, who had some 146 business to take care of and had disappeared. I was pointed to the canteen by the operations assistants, which I duly found. I wandered in and joined the queue, amongst all of the factory engineers, and when I sat down – for what must have literally been a matter of seconds – a lady came scuttling across to me and said, "Sir, are you one of the pilots?" I promptly replied in the affirmative. "Well, sir," she said, "if you would like to follow me, I will take you to the pilot's mess."

I could not believe what I was hearing. It was such a massive culture shock, having worked for BCal where the canteen was frequented by everyone from pilots to cabin crew, office workers and engineers. I looked around and could see I was the centre of attention . . . "That is very kind of you," I replied, "but if you don`t mind I am quite happy here," and stayed put. There was no way I was going to walk out and eat in the pilot's mess.

All airfields are unique.

Filton at Bristol, home of the Concorde development, was heavily involved with Airbus, as was Hawarden (pronounced 'Hardin') near Chester.

Woodford was the main flight test development centre, and it was where I spent a lot of time flying with the test pilots as part of the development program for the 125-1000. In addition, 146 and Nimrod development was taking place.

Warton was home of the Typhoon Eurofighter development.

Hatfield was home for Bae commercial aircraft, and all of the marketing and sales teams appeared to be based there for the 146 and 125 product lines.

Prestwick was Jetstream 31 and 41 development, and ATP, as well as production and flight test.

Apart from the odd flight on a 146, under flight test conditions out of Woodford, I predominately flew the 125, which was being re-branded under Bae Corporate Jets. The flying was extremely varied, including 'comms' flying, which involved operating shuttles all over the UK for Bae as well as to Toulouse in France. This connected all of the sites and was run like a mini private airline.

There were different shuttle schedules, but you would typically fly Hatfield, Hawarden (Chester),

Filton, Hawarden in the morning, and then do the reverse in the afternoon as a 'split duty'. Or you could fly Hatfield, Woodford (Manchester), Prestwick, again doing the reverse, or fly Hatfield to Filton (Bristol) to night stop, and then the next morning operate a shuttle to Toulouse, which is the Airbus Industries headquarters.

On top of that we were allocated 'demonstration tours', where we would go to a region with an aircraft and a sales team for what could be protracted periods of time. My first tour was to the United States in July of that year, and I flew with Bae Inc American pilots who were based in Washington, initially at Manassas in Virginia but then latterly at Washington Dulles International.

Ferry flights involved taking brand-new aircraft that were 'off test' from Hawarden across to the completion centre in Little Rock Arkansas.

The ferry flights were extremely challenging, but tremendously enjoyable, because the aircraft were 'green'. That is to say they were just 'shells' in green primer, with no interiors. We had thermal blankets hanging behind us, with nothing but bare aircraft that looked like the interior of World War II bombers. Crates of spares and equipment, survival gear, sandwiches, thermos flasks and pee bottles were provided!

The aircraft had basic ferry kits, with a single VLF/Omega navigation kit that would be disconnected and boxed back up for us to carry back to the UK;

but the biggest piece of equipment that was missing was an autopilot and yaw damper! Boy, did it sharpen your flying skills, as we would hand fly in instrument meteorological conditions, through the weather across 'the pond', at high altitude!

Because we could not enter the organised North Atlantic track system, we would route initially out of Hawarden to Keflavik in Iceland, where we would top off the tanks to fly non–stop on the old World War II ferry route to Bangor, Maine. In the war, aircraft were ferried to the UK along this very route over Greenland. Upon arrival at Bangor, the aircraft would 'technically' be imported overnight into the United States. This was all handled by the agents.

We would spend the night in the airport Hilton and, if the weather allowed, venture in a taxi down to Captain Nick`s for seafood dinners. I can testify just how cold Bangor could be in the winter!

The following morning we would again hand fly to Little Rock Arkansas, where we would hand the aircraft over to the completion centre. Positioning home as passengers was nearly always through Dallas Fort Worth. (I would often take advantage of days off in the Dallas Fort Worth area, catching up with family friends.)

The thing with the 125 from a flying perspective is that it did not have hydraulic servo controls, and even though control harmony was commensurate with speed and altitude, it took tremendous effort to stay at assigned altitudes, especially when you picked up standing waves over Greenland, for example. Clear air turbulence (CAT) would be exhausting and then, at the end of it, you had to hand fly an approach on raw data, because that is all you had!

But I had some superb mentors, and the likes of Chris Shrimpton, Chris Follows, Neil Smith and, of course, John Horscroft led by example, and would keep on speed and at altitude all the way across. What it taught me was the importance of pacing yourself on some of those long, gruelling days.

On the day of the ferry there would inevitably be delays due to paperwork and, on occasion, simply because we were waiting for the Customs officer from Liverpool to show up at Hawarden to release us. Getting wound up did not help, and you simply had to just go with the flow. There was always a cut-off point time-wise, and if it had to be delayed to the next morning, then so be it.

There was only one occasion when we had to implement plan B, and that was with John Horscroft, when we flew from Hawarden to Narsarsuaq in southern Greenland and then onto Bangor with an 800 series ferry flight. The aircraft was then delivered to Wichita, Kansas the following day.

The weather was appalling, and the turbulence flying in and out of Narsarsuaq bone-jarring. Indeed, the couple of attempts I made to photograph the glacier at the end of the valley during climb out just show a blur of snow, ice and rock!

I remember the low cloud put us right on the limits flying into Wichita, and John, who was flying the sector, kept it nailed all the way down, breaking out of the cloud base exactly where we should have been, within a foot and within a knot. John was originally a helicopter test pilot, and I have never seen anyone so gifted in the art of flying. He never said a word all the way down the approach, epitomising the 'steely-eyed test pilot' of folklore.

The cold in the flight deck was without doubt the biggest challenge on the ferry flights. I used to wear layers and layers of clothing, including thermals and extra socks. Neil Smith found a unique way of being able to hoist his legs up onto the instrument combing and place his feet on the front windscreens, that were electrically heated. Not when he was flying the sector, I hasten to add!

On occasion I would find myself, after a ferry flight, being asked to support Bae Inc with a demo trip or additional flying tasks, including flying military variants that took me to some obscure development sites. Enough said.

The demos were always exciting, though, and you never knew from week to week where you were going to end up or who with. One afternoon, I found myself with Mason Morgan, a Bae Inc pilot, taking a demonstrator to Barbados out of Washington. The following day we continued oceanic down the east side of South America to Brazil, where we spent a period of time operating a series of demonstration flights.

Demo tours were also exhaustive, covering vast regions and numerous challenges. The first long tour I undertook was to the Far East, and we left Hatfield on the 5th May 1991 with a 125-800 demonstrator and a salesman. (Regional sales teams would join us as we progressed.)

First stop was Luxor, and a static display before continuing to Dubai.

The following day took us through India and on to Kuala Lumpur (KL), the capital of Malaysia. We stayed in KL for a number of days, flying several passenger demonstrations. These were always straightforward, as our job was to keep it as if it were on rails and let the sales team work their magic.

Pilot demos were quite another thing, however, especially if you had passengers, and managing expectations was the key to a successful flight. The pilot would want to see maximum rates of climb, steep turns at altitude, for example, and you had to be mindful that the people in the cabin had no desire to experience any of that at all! As a rule, we always tried to separate out pilot demos from passenger demonstrations, for obvious reasons, especially if a customer pilot was taking a seat at the controls!

The challenge with the passenger demo flights would more often than not be airspace and air traffic constraints within the country we flew. In Russia, for example, they would often put a 'navigator' onboard to keep an eye on us. There were no navigators in Malaysia, though, just spectacular countryside and jungle, with a thunderstorm every afternoon to liven things up. (The heat and humidity made eating out in the evenings an experience in its own right!)

We flew to Ipoh and back on the 8th May, and after several more demo flights left the next day for Jakarta, where we spent a week. From there on to Kota Kinabalu in the Malaysian state of Sabah (Northern Borneo), where we flew for several days in and out of some pretty strange places.

One lunchtime we arrived at an air strip that had originally been a Japanese World War II base. It had metal planking with asphalt poured over it to form a hard standing. We were taken to an old colonial country club, where all the waiters were dressed in tropical whites. Outside was an old Morris Minor that looked as if it had just come off the production line. It was as if the clock had been wound back fifty years and everyone was so pleased that the British were back. There was barely a soul to be seen, and it was eerily quiet as we ate an *a la carte* lunch looking out over a spectacular bay surrounded by jungle.

From Kota Kinabalu we positioned the aircraft to Manila in the Philippines, which I found pretty seedy if I'm honest. The hotel was awash with prostitutes, and even the flights we undertook were questionable.

I struggled on occasions to understand who the good guys were and who the bad guys were. I appreciate we were just the pilots and it was up to the sales teams to work out who was who, but I couldn't help but feel some of the potential customers were taking advantage of our hospitality and had no intention of ever placing orders. Having said that, there were orders placed as a result of the tour, but when and by whom was none of our business and it was something we were (quite rightly) separated from.

From Manila to Seoul, South Korea, and a couple of days flying three demo trips before continuing on to Beijing, China. Beijing was fascinating, and I am so glad we got to see it before the tremendous economic growth and power house developed that is China of today. I have never seen so many bikes! Everyone cycled. On our days off we were taken to the Great Wall.

From Beijing we flew south to Guangzhou on the Chinese mainland, and after a few days to Bangkok. Bangkok, for some bizarre reason, I did not find seedy! The Thai people were extremely friendly and, certainly to me, always seemed to be smiling. I spent as much time as I could exploring the canals and visiting temples. We flew internally within Thailand and eventually headed west for Hatfield via Bombay (modern-day Mumbai) in India and Iraklion, Greece. We arrived back in Hatfield on 2nd June, a month after leaving.

As well as demonstration flights and shuttle comms flights I would often be allocated to Hawarden to work with the resident test pilots Tony Craig and John Sadler, both ex-military pilots and tasked, along with the flight test engineers, to take aircraft from 'first flight' through the production flight test schedule to being released 'off test'.

The portacabins at '2 Site', where flight test was based, became my home from home, and I have fond memories of working there with the railway line to North Wales running beside us, separating us from the Dee Estuary. Diesel locomotives and being mothered by Agnes, the PA who had a wicked sense of humour and always made sure there were digestives in the biscuit tin for tea breaks, make for fond memories.

The facilities were like most British Aerospace sites at the time – archaic and a mixture of leftover war surplus hangars and buildings. Except, however, on the other side of the airfield, where a modern factory co-existed, building wings for Airbus Industries, which it continues to do to this day.

The flying was superb, and on test flights we would either head up to Scotland or out over the Irish Sea to work within a box of airspace and occupy block altitudes. The rain was relentless, though, and I remember rubbing condensation off the window in the tearoom, looking across at the hills in Wales, and Agnes saying, "That's just one big weather machine that Wales, you know!" She was right, and there is nothing worse than a cold wet airfield in the middle of winter; it's miserable, and due to the geographical nature of the United Kingdom, the northwest tends to get hammered.

As well as Hawarden, I would also spend time at Woodford on secondment, where development flight test took place. (More of that later.)

There were many flights and many experiences that I will cherish from my time with Bae. Undoubtedly, one of the highlights not just for the period of time at Bae but for my career as a whole was when Peter Tait, the test pilot who flew the Mosquito based at Hawarden, casually asked if I would like to fly with him on a sortie in August 1991. It was a bit like asking someone if the Pope is Catholic? Of course I did! As a result, I found myself in the right-hand seat of RR299 (G-ASKH) with Peter at Hatfield. I was duly put in charge of map reading and the manifold pressure!

It was to be a busy day, as we were tasked to take off and initially form up with a Shorts Skyvan that was being used for air-to-air photography. As we climbed up and met the other aircraft on station, I could see the rear ramp was down and a photographer in a harness was hanging out the back. With a dearth of hand signals and arm waving, we would position into various quadrants for the photographer, Norman Pealing.

The pictures that came out were superb, and one ended up on the front cover of *Pilot* magazine in January 1992. Inside was a superb article written by Peter Henley, and many more of the pictures taken that day.

As soon as the photo shoot was completed we were waved off and, with no navigation instruments, we charged off to North Wales and the coast, where we ran along the shoreline towards Anglesey. I was desperately trying to follow our course with a topographical chart and pretend I knew exactly where we were! What I do remember however is caravans. Thousands of them, all along the coast!

Timing was critical, and we circled just off the coast before being called in to commence a flying display at RAF Valley, which Peter executed on cue.

I remember looking down at the Royal Air Force Red Arrows lined up on the side as we thundered down the centre line before pulling up . . . and started the display with what was basically a series of wingovers. The old girl needed to be treated with a huge amount of respect and certainly was too precious to be abused!

From Anglesey it was not far back to Hawarden, where the wind had picked up, and Peter quite rightly chose the short crosswind runway to get us as much as possible into wind. The Mosquito had previously been involved in an incident, damaging the undercarriage, and with such poor directional control available on takeoff and landing, into wind was always the preferred option.

Safely back at Hawarden, and with the Mosquito back in the hangar, I remember looking up and thinking, *I can`t believe I just did that. What a day!*

It did not end there, however, because Peter felt, quite rightly, when we had driven back to Hatfield that evening in a rental car, that we should have a pint in the pub just outside the perimeter – and proceeded to continue the conversation we had had in the car, about flying!

Politics, which will also be covered later, was a significant part of any company's existence, and in 1993, when it was clear that Corporate Jets, which is what Bae Commercial Aircraft had morphed into, was being sold and shipped to the States, it was time for me to leave.

I had joined Bae thinking it would provide stability and a career. Whilst it did not end up that way, what it did provide me with was experience – and an incredible experience that would stay with me for the rest of my life. To all the men and women in every capacity at Hatfield, Filton, Hawarden, Woodford, Prestwick and Warton . . . thank you!

On the 11th October 1993 I joined Virgin Atlantic Airways.

Chapter 10

10 to the -9

10 to the -9 is the factor aircraft designers build into calculations in order to protect against failures. What this means in layman's terms is that there is a 1 in 10,000,000,000 chance of something catastrophic happening.[13]

Throughout my career, for some inexplicable reason, it is these 1 in 10,000,000,000 events that I have found myself having to deal with . . . aircraft, and the components that make up the myriads of systems within, tend not to always follow the protocol.

In addition to designing in system safety factors, system redundancy and extensive testing and certification, a manufacturer will produce 'abnormal' and 'emergency' checklists that will

---

[13] At the time of writing, this prerequisite is being investigated extensively as part of the investigations into the 2018 and 2019 fatal accidents of the Boeing 737 Max 8.

allow the operator to follow a preordained path of identifying and dealing with any problem that may occur.

It is quite simple really. An engine failure occurs, which leads you to carry out the recall or memory items followed by a checklist: aviate, navigate and communicate whilst managing the checklist, and the aircraft lands safely without incident. Easy.

Or at least that is the theory.

When the crew of a Hawaiian B737 of Aloha Airlines found the top of their aircraft had unpeeled in flight, they departed from altitude . . . towards the Pacific Ocean. Suddenly they had a convertible, for which there was no checklist.

Over Iowa in the United States, the crew of a DC-10 lost all of their hydraulics as a result of an engine disc failure cutting like a chainsaw through the back of the aircraft. Control was achieved purely by differential thrust, and the manipulation of the thrust levers powering the remaining wing-mounted engines, the flying control surfaces having been rendered useless from the loss of hydraulic fluid to power their respective actuators.

The most well-known incident recently, that in theory 'could not happen', was the Hudson River arrival as the result of significant thrust loss to both engines of an A320 through coming into contact with a flock of Canada geese.

None of these incidents contained checklists for the events, or had formed part of recurrent training up to that date. 1 in 10,000,000,000.

And yet, despite the odds of these events even occurring in the first place, they did occur, and it was the skill and dedication of the individuals involved that resulted in lives being saved. (The first two events described did, sadly, have fatalities, but the events when they occurred were, in theory, not survivable for anyone onboard.)

Any line pilot will tell you that it is these and other non-conforming failures or problems that are at the core to good airmanship; yet 'airmanship' is a catch-all phrase that covers everything that generally identifies a pilot exercising his or her knowledge and understanding of complex situations that have positive outcomes, from taking good decisions with respect to the weather, flight planning or aircraft handling.

Threat and error management is a tool which can be applied to capture identified threats and errors. What you in effect do is 'trap' the threats and errors, not allowing them to result in an undesirable outcome (i.e. a crash!). One of the best examples of this is playing the 'what if' game at different phases of flight, and even before leaving the ground:

What if an engine fails at a critical moment climbing out of this valley with mountains and thunderstorms to the south?

What if we depressurise now over Greenland?

What if there is a fire in the cabin right now and we can't put it out? The nearest airport is 500 miles away. Do we put the aircraft down on a gravel strip that is 4,000 feet long below us over Northern Canada, and accept we will go off the end at 50mph and the aircraft breaks into three at the production joints? Some people will survive, some won't. Or do we just sit here throwing fire extinguishers at it when we know it has got a hold and will not go out, toxic fumes are filling the cabin, and people are hammering on the locked cockpit door whilst we breathe oxygen . . . until, that is, the fire burns through the structure and we all die at the point of impact in the perma-frost below just as we reach terminal velocity.

Tough decisions.

None more so than on the flight deck of an Alaskan Airlines MD-80 just off the Pacific Coast of Los Angeles in January 2000. The aeroplane's screw jack – that controlled the horizontal stabiliser – had malfunctioned. The reasons for this, and the actions of both the airline and crew, are detailed extensively in the NTSB report. It was most harrowing for me, as a pilot, reading the cockpit voice recorder transcript, where the pilots try to 'work the problem' all the way down to the point of impact with the sea.

The following transcript is from Alaskan 261 as published by the NTSB.

RDO – *Radio transmission from accident aircraft, Alaska 261*

CAM – *Cockpit area microphone voice or sound source*

PA – *Voice or sound heard on the public address system channel*

HOT – *Hot microphone voice or sound source 1*

For RDO, CAM, HOT, and PA comments:

-**1** – *Voice identified as the captain*

-**2** – *Voice identified as the first officer*

-**3** – *Voice identified as a flight attendant*

-**?** – *Voice unidentified*

MZT – *Radio transmission from Mazetlan Center*

LAX CTR1 – *Radio transmission from the Los Angeles Air Route Traffic Control Center sector 30 controller*

LAX CTR2 – *Radio transmission from the Los Angeles Air Route Traffic Control Center sector 25 controller*

LAX-MX – *Radio transmission from Alaska Airlines Maintenance facility in Los Angeles*

LAX-OPS – *Radio transmission from Alaska Airlines Operations facility in Los Angeles*

SEA-DIS – *Radio transmission from Alaska Airlines Dispatch facility in Seattle*

SEA-MX – *Radio transmission from Alaska*

Airlines maintenance facility in Seattle

-1 – *First voice*

-2 – *Second voice*

ATIS – *Radio transmission from Los Angeles airport Automated Terminal Information System*

CAWS – *Mechanical voice or sound source from the Central Aural Warning System, as heard on the Cockpit Area Microphone channel.*

* – *Unintelligible word*

@ – *Non-pertinent word*

– *Expletive*

- - - - – *Break in continuity or interruption in comment*

( ) – *Questionable insertion*

[ ] – *Editorial insertion*

... – *Pause*

TIME - SOURCE - CONTENT

1607:51 LAX-MX-1 and two sixty one maintenance.

1607:53 RDO-1 two sixty one go.

1607:54 LAX-MX-1 yea are you guys with the uh, horizontal situation?

1607:58 RDO-1 affirmative.

1607:59 LAX-MX-1 yea did you try the suitcase handles and the pickle switches right?

1608:03 RDO-1 yea we tried everything together, uh...

1608:08 RDO-1 ...we've run just about everything, if you've got any hidden circuit breakers we'd love to know about 'em.

1608:14 LAX-MX-1 I'm off. I'll look at the uh circuit breaker uh guide just as a double check and um yea I just wanted to know if you tried the pickle switches and the suitcase handles to see if it was movin in with any of the uh other switches other than the uh suitcase handles alone or nothing.

1608:29.9 RDO-1 yea we tried just about every iteration.

1608:32 LAX-MX-1 and alternate's inop too, huh?

1608:35.1 RDO-1 yup, it's just it appears to be jammed, the uh the whole thing, it spikes out when we use the primary, we get AC load that tells me the motor's tryin to run but the brake won't move it, when we use the alternate, nothing happens.

1608:50 LAX-MX-1 ok and you you you say you get a spike when on the meter up there in the cockpit when you uh try to move it with the uh um with the primary right?

1608:59 CAM-1 I'm gonna click it off, you got it.

1609:00 CAM-2 ok.

1609:01.5 RDO-1 affirmative, we get a spike when we do the primary trim but there's no appreciable uh change in the uh electrical uh when we do the alternate.

1609:09 LAX-MX-1 ok thank you sir see you here.

1609:11 RDO-1 ok.

1609:13 CAM-1 let's do that.

1609:14.8 CAM [sound of click]

1609:14.8 CAM-1 this'll click it off.

1609:16 CAM [sound of clunk]

1609:16.9 CAM [sound of two faint thumps in short succession]

1609:17.0 CAWS [sound similar to horizontal stabilizer-in-motion audible tone]

1609:18 CAM-1 holy #.

1609:19.6 CAWS [sound similar to horizontal stabilizer-in-motion audible tone]

1609:21 CAM-1 you got it?... # me.

1609:24 CAM-2 what are you doin?

1609:25 CAM-1 I it clicked off---

1609:25.4 CAWS [sound of chime] Altitude

1609:26 CAM-1 ---it * got worse... ok.

1609:30 CAM [sound similar to airframe vibration begins]

1609:31 CAM-1 you're stalled.

1609:32 CAM [sound similar to airframe vibration becomes louder]

1609:33 CAM-1 no no you gotta release it ya gotta release it.

1609:34 CAM [sound of click]

1609:34 CAM [sound similar to airframe vibration ends]

1609:42.4 CAM-1 let's * speedbrake.

1609:46 CAM-1 gimme a high pressure pumps.

1609:52 CAM-2 ok

1609:52 CAM-1 help me back help me back.

1609:54 CAM-2 ok.

1609:55 RDO-1 center Alaska two sixty one we are uh in a dive here.

1610:01.6 RDO-1 and I've lost control, vertical pitch.

1610:01.9 CAWS [sound of clacker] Overspeed. (begins and repeats for approx 33 seconds)

1610:05 LAX-CTR1 Alaska two sixty one say again sir.

1610:06.6 RDO-1 yea were out of twenty six thousand feet, we are in a vertical dive... not a dive yet... but uh we've lost vertical control of our airplane.

1610:15 CAM [sound of click]

1610:20 CAM-1 just help me.

1610:22 CAM-1 once we get the speed slowed maybe... we'll be ok.

1610:28.2 RDO-1 we're at twenty three seven request uh.

1610:33 RDO-1 yea we got it back under control here.

1610:34 RDO-2 no we don't, ok.

1610:37 CAM-1 ok.

1610:37 LAX-CTR1 the altitude you'd like to uh to remain at?

1610:40 CAM [sound of click]

*1610:45 CAM-2 let's take the speedbrakes off I'm * ---*

1610:46 CAM-1 no no leave them there. it seems to be helping.

1610:51 CAM-1 # me.

1610:53 CAWS [sound of chime] Altitude

1610:55 CAM-1 ok it really wants to pitch down.

1610:58 CAM-2 ok.

1610:59 CAM-1 don't mess with that.

1611:04 CAM-2 I agree with you.

1611:04 LAX-CTR1 Alaska two sixty one say your condition.

1611:06.6 RDO-1 two sixty one we are at twenty four thousand feet, kinda stabilized.

1611:10 RDO-1 we're slowing here, and uh, we're gonna uh.

1611:15 RDO-1 do a little troubleshooting, can you gimme a block between uh, twenty and twenty five?

1611:21 LAX-CTR1 Alaska two sixty one maintain block altitude flight level two zero zero through flight level two five zero.

1611:27 RDO-1 Alaska two sixty one we'll take that block we'll be monitor'n the freq.

1611:31 CAM-2 you have the airplane, let me just try it.

1611:33 CAM-1 ok.

1611:33 CAM-2 uh how hard is it?

1611:33 CAM-1 I don't know, my adrenaline's goin ... it was really tough there for a while.

1611:38 CAM-2 yea it is.

1611:39 CAM-1 ok.

1611:43 CAM-2 whatever we did is no good, don't do that again.

1611:44 CAM-1 yea, no it went down, it went to full nose down.

1611:48 CAM-2 uh it's a lot worse than it was?

1611:50 CAM-1 yea yea we're in much worse shape now.

1611:59 CAM-1 I think it's at the stop, full stop... and I'm thinking, we can- can it go any worse... but it probably can... but when we slowed down, let's slow it let's get down to two hundred knots and see what happens.

1612:16 CAM-2 ok?

1612:16 CAM [sound of click]

1612:17 CAM-2 we have to put the slats out and everything... flaps and slats.

1612:20 CAM-1 yea... well we'll wait ok, you got it for a second?

1612:23 CAM-2 yea.

1612:25.3 RDO-1 maintenance two sixty one are you on?

1612:30 LAX-MX-2 yea two sixty one this is maintenance.

1612:32.0 RDO-1 ok we did---

1612:33.2 RDO-1 ---we did both the pickle switch and the suitcase handles and it ran away full nose trim down.

1612:39 LAX-MX-2 oh it ran away trim down.

*1612:42 RDO-1 and now we're in a * pinch so we're holding, uh we're worse than we were.*

1612:50 LAX-MX-2 ok uh... geez.

1612:52 LAX-MX-1 you want me to talk to em? (in the background during previous transmission)

1612:55 LAX-MX-1 yea two sixty one maintenance uh uh

you getting full nose trim down but are you getting any you don't get no nose trim up is that correct?

1613:04 RDO-1 that's affirm, we went to full nose down and I'm afraid to try it again to see if we can get it to go in the other direction.

1613:10 LAX-MX-1 ok well your discretion uh if you want to try it, that's ok with me, if not that's fine. um we'll see you at the gate.

1613:20 CAM-2 did it happen when in reverse? when you pulled back it went forward?

1613:22 CAM-1 I went tab down... right, and it should have come back instead it went the other way.

1613:29 CAM-2 uh huh.

1613:30 CAM-1 what do you think?

1613:32 CAM-2 uhhh.

1613:32 CAM-1 you wanna try it or not?

1613:32 CAM-2 uhh no, boy I don't know.

1613:33 CAM-1 it's up to you man.

1613:35 CAM-2 let's head back toward uh here, let's see... well we're---

1613:39 CAM-1 I like where were goin out over the water myself... I don't like goin this fast though.

1613:50 CAM [sound of click]

1613:57 CAM-1 ok you got * [sound similar to short interruption in recording] second?

1613:58 CAM-2 yea.

1613:59 CAM-2 we better... talk to the people in the back there.

1614:03 CAM-1 yea I know.

1614:04 LAX-CTR1 Alaska two sixty one let me know if you need anything.

1614:08 RDO-2 yea we're still workin this.

1614:12 PA-1 folks we have had a flight control problem up front here, we're workin it, uh that's Los Angeles off to the right there, that's where we're intending to go, we're pretty busy up here workin this situation. I don't anticipate any big problems once we get a couple of sub systems on the line. but we will be going into L A X and I'd anticipate us parking there in about twenty to thirty minutes.

1614:39 CAM-1 ok... did the, first of all, speedbrakes, did they have any effect?

1614:49 CAM-1 let's put the power where it'll be for one point two, for landing. you buy that?

1614:53 CAM-1 slow it down and see what happens.

1614:54 LAX-CTR1 Alaska two sixty one contact L A center one two six point five two they are aware of your situation.

1615:00.0 RDO-2 ok Alaska two sixty one say again the frequency, one two zero five two?

1615:02 CAM-1 I got the yoke.

1615:04 LAX-CTR1 Alaska two sixty one, twenty six fifty two.

1615:06 RDO-2 thank you.

1615:07 LAX-CTR1 you're welcome have a good day.

1615:19.7 RDO-2 L A Alaska two sixty one we're with

you, we're at twenty two five, we have a jammed stabilizer and we're maintaining altitude with difficulty, uh but uh we can maintain altitude we think... and our intention is to land at Los Angeles.

1615:36 LAX-CTR2 Alaska two sixty one L A center roger um you're cleared to Los Angeles airport via present position direct uh Santa Monica, direct Los Angeles and uh, you want lower now or what do you want to do sir?

1615:54 CAM-1 let me get let me have it.

1615:56 RDO-1 center uh Alaska two sixty one. I need to get down about ten, change my configuration, make sure I can control the jet and I'd like to do that out here over the bay if I may.

1616:07 LAX-CTR2 ok Alaska two sixty one roger that standby here.

1616:11 CAM-2 let's do it at this altitude instead---

1616:11 CAM-1 what?

1616:12 CAM-2 ---of goin to ten let's do it at this altitude.

1616:14 CAM-1 cause the airflow's that much difference down at ten, this air's thin enough that that you know what I'm sayin?

1616:20 CAM-2 yea uh I'll tell em to uh---

1616:22 CAM-1 I just made a PA to everyone to get everybody---

1616:24 CAM-2 ok.

1616:26 CAM-1 ---down you might call the flight attendants.

1616:27 CAM [sound similar to cockpit door operating]

1616:32 CAM-3 I was just comin up this way.

1616:32 LAX-CTR2 Alaska two sixty one fly a heading of two eight zero and descend and maintain one seven thousand.

1616:34 CAM-2 uhh.

1616:36 CAM [sound similar to cockpit door operating]

1616:39.0 RDO-1 two eight zero and one seven seventeen thousand Alaska two sixty one. and we generally need a block altitude.

1616:45 LAX-CTR2 ok and just um I tell you what do that for now sir, and contact L A center on one three five point five, they'll have further uhh instructions for you sir.

1616:56.9 RDO-2 ok thirty five five say the altimeter setting?

1616:59 LAX-CTR2 the L A altimeter is three zero one eight.

1617:01 CAM-1 I need everything picked up---

1617:02 RDO-2 thank you.

1617:02 CAM-1 ---and everybody strapped down---

1617:04 CAM-3 ok.

1617:04 CAM-1 ---cause I'm gonna unload the airplane and see if we can---

1617:06 CAM-3 ok.

1617:07 CAM-1 ---we can regain control of it that way.

1617:09 CAM-3 ok we had like a big bang back there---

1617:11 CAM-1 yea I heard it---

1617:12 CAM-3 ok.

1617:12 CAM-1 ---the stab trim I think it---

1617:13 CAM-2 you heard it in the back?

1617:13 CAM-3 yea.

1617:14 CAM-2 yea.

1617:15 CAM-3 so---

1617:15 CAM-1 I think the stab trim thing is broke---

1617:17 CAM-3 ---I didn't wanna call you guys... but---

1617:18 CAM-1 no no that's good.

1617:20 CAM-3 ---that girl, they're like, you better go up there---

1617:21 CAM-1 I need you everybody strapped in now, dear.

1617:22 CAM-3 ---and tell them.

1617:23 CAM-3 ok.

1617:24 CAM-1 cause I'm gonna I'm going to release the back pressure and see if I can get it... back.

1617:30 CAM [sound similar to cockpit door operating]

1617:33 CAM-2 three zero one eight.

1617:37 CAM-1 I'll get it here.

1617:40 CAM-2 I don't think you want any more speedbrakes do you?

1617:42 CAM-1 uhh no, actually.

1617:46 CAM-2 he wants us to maintain seventeen.

1617:51 CAM-1 ok I need help with this here.

1617:52 CAM-1 slats ext... let's---

1617:54 CAM-2 ok slats---

1617:54 CAM-1 gimme slats extend.

1617:55 CAM-2 got it.

1617:56.6 CAM [sound similar to slat/flap handle movement]

1617:58 CAM-1 I'm test flyin now---

1617:59 CAM-2 how does it feel?

1618:00 CAM-1 it's wantin to pitch over more on you.

1618:02 CAM-2 really?

1618:03 CAM-1 yea.

1618:04 CAM-2 try flaps?... fifteen, eleven?

1618:05 CAM-1 ahh let's go to eleven.

1618:07.3 CAM [sound similar to slat/flap handle movement]

1618:09 CAM-2 ok... get some power on.

1618:10 CAM-1 I'm at two hundred and fifty knots, so I'm lookin...

1618:17 CAM-2 real hard?

1618:17 CAM-1 no actually it's pretty stable right here... see but we got to get down to a hundred an eighty.

1618:26 CAM-1 OK... bring bring the flaps and slats back up for me.

1618:32 CAM-2 slats too?

1618:33 CAM-1 yea.

1618:36.8 CAM [sound similar to slat/flap handle movement]

1618:37 CAM-2 that gives us... twelve thousand pounds of fuel, don't over boost them.

1618:47 CAM-1 what I'm what I wanna do...

1618:48 CAM [sound similar to slat/flap handle movement]

1618:49 CAM-1 is get the nose up... and then let the nose fall through and see if we can stab it when it's unloaded.

1618:54 CAWS [sound of chime] Altitude (repeats for approximately 34 seconds)

1618:56 CAM-2 you mean use this again? I don't think we should... if it can fly, it's like---

1619:01 CAM-1 it's on the stop now, it's on the stop.

1619:04 CAM-2 well not according to that it's not.

1619:07 CAM-2 the trim might be, and then it might be uh, if something's popped back there---

1619:11 CAM-1 yea.

1619:11 CAM-2 ---it might be * mechanical damage too.

1619:14 CAM-2 I think if it's controllable, we oughta just try to land it---

1619:16 CAM-1 you think so? ok let's head for L A.

1619:21.1 CAM [sound of faint thump]

1619:24 CAM-2 you feel that?

1619:25 CAM-1 yea.

1619:29 CAM-1 ok gimme sl--- see, this is a bitch.

1619:31 CAM-2 is it?

1619:31 CAM-1 yea.

1619:32.8 CAM [sound of two clicks similar to slat/flap handle movement]

1619:36 CAM-? *

1619:36.6 CAM [sound of extremely loud noise] [increase in background noise begins and continues to end of recording] [sound similar to loose articles moving around in cockpit]

*1619:37 CAM-? ***

1619:37.6 PA [sound similar to CVR startup tone]

1619:43 CAM-2 mayday.

1619:49 CAM-1 push and roll, push and roll.

1619:54 CAM-1 ok, we are inverted... and now we gotta get it....

1619:59 CAM [sound of chime]

*1620:03 CAM-1 kick ***

1620:04 CAM-1 push push push... push the blue side up.

1620:14 CAM-1 push.

1620:14 CAM-2 I'm pushing.

1620:16 CAM-1 ok now let's kick rudder... left rudder left rudder.

1620:18 CAM-2 I can't reach it.

1620:20 CAM-1 ok right rudder... right rudder.

1620:25 CAM-1 are we flyin?... we're flyin... we're flyin... tell 'em what we're doin.

*1620:33 CAM-2 oh yea let me get ***

*1620:35 CAM-1 ***

1620:38 CAM-1 gotta get it over again... at least upside down we're flyin.

1620:40.6 PA [sound similar to CVR start-up tone]

*1620:42 CAM-? ***

*1620:44 CAM-? ***

1620:49 CAM [sounds similar to compressor stalls begin and continue to end of recording]

1620:49 CAM [sound similar to engine spool down]

1620:54 CAM-1 speedbrakes.

1620:55.1 CAM-2 got it.
1620:56.2 CAM-1 ah here we go.
1620:57.1 [end of recording]

End of transcript.
https://www.ntsb.gov/investigations/
AccidentReports/Reports/AAR0201.pdf

For any pilot, 'there but for the grace of god go I . . .' It is harrowing to read, and even more harrowing to view on the internet when coupled with the animation from the flight data recorder.

Death is there, in the background, and no matter how you try to dress it up and surround it with comfort blankets it is still there, waiting for you to either be in the wrong place at the wrong time, or to simply screw up. If you do screw up, it will get you, and sadly some people lose their lives because they step out of the flight envelope for whatever reason and get caught out. Rules in aviation are there for a damn-good reason, essentially to stop you and others from getting killed, but I have also witnessed a life being lost simply because they were in the wrong place at the wrong time. This I can get my head around, as it is something we have little or no control over as individuals.

The best analogy is that of being in a well-built brand-new car with the latest safety devices, driving within one mile an hour of the speed limit, spaced sensibly from the car in front . . . and the bridge you are driving over collapses into the valley below, taking you and the other cars and trucks on the bridge to your death. No time to call loved ones or reflect on a lifetime journey. You are 2.5 seconds from death. Exactly this scenario happened in Genoa, Italy, in 2018.

There is a picture of the cars at the edge of the Genoa bridge collapse that managed to stop in time. Can you imagine the conversation they had with their families that night?

1 in 10,000,000,000.

Chapter 11

Cause and Effect

When people put themselves and others in danger it makes me mad as hell. There are good reasons for regulations and standard operating procedures as, on a whole, they keep you and everyone around you safe and, most importantly, alive.

In 1987 I returned from a period of flying in Texas to the UK, and in the November I was undertaking instrument rating training at Stansted Airport just north of London. Whilst in Texas I had been flying a 55 Beech Baron[14] all over the state, and as far afield as New Mexico and Nevada.

I loved that aeroplane. No ordinary aeroplane, as previously mentioned it had a Colemill conversion which installed two 300hp engines and gave it the performance of a mountain goat – extremely useful for flying in hot and high conditions in the

---

[14] When I converted onto the aircraft, I flew extensively with an experienced and fully qualified Beech Baron pilot.

southwestern states. The caveat, however, was that you had to treat it with respect and the 'blue line', which was the minimum controllable airspeed in the event of an engine failure, was sacrosanct: you did not let the aircraft go below that speed or you would lose directional control, with the remaining 300hp engine working against you.

In December of that year word got back to me that the aircraft, having been sold, had crashed, killing the new owner and the instructor on their first flight.

Why?

The aircraft had dual controls and, as a qualified multi-engine instructor, I would often fly in the right-hand seat with the aircraft owners. I had accumulated a lot of hours on that aircraft and knew it well. Yes, it was a handful, but a lot of high performance complex twin engine aircraft are. What on earth had happened?

Eventually the National Transportation Safety Board published the accident report and the narrative reads as follows:

> 'The purpose of the flight was to satisfy an insurance requirement that the owner receive 10 hours dual instruction in this aircraft. The dual controls had been removed and the single control was on the left side. The aircraft was observed in a clockwise flat spin up to impact.

The landing gear was down as were the flaps. The left engine was at full power while the right throttle was in the idle position and the propeller control was in the feather position. The propeller was against the start lock pins. No malfunctions were found. The CFI, who was in the right seat had .5 hrs of flight time in Beech 95-B55s. FAR's prohibit the CFI from acting as the PIC in multiengine acft without dual controls installed.'

https://app.ntsb.gov/pdfgenerator/ReportGeneratorFile.ashx?EventID=20001213X32528&AKey=1&RType=-Final&IType=FA

'No malfunctions were found . . .'

I went from feeling sick to angry, to very angry. It transpired that the aircraft broker had swapped the dual controls for a single yoke prior to the sale (the dual controls being valuable presumably as a re-sale item). The instructor, who had .5 hours on type (probably not the 300hp version), and the new owner, who had 0.0 hours experience on type, went out and did single engine training in violation of federal aviation regulations that forbid any form of instruction without dual controls. An absolute tragedy for their families, and a tragedy for aviation . . . and an accident that simply should never have happened.

Whilst at British Aerospace we sadly lost pilots, and even after I left to embark on a long-haul airline career loss of life continued.

Russell was a very unassuming, pleasant person to be around; and seven years my younger, he was the epitome of what we on this side of the Atlantic would consider to be 'a decent chap'. (Aviation does, on occasion, attract loud, larger than life rambunctious characters. Russell was not one of them.) The last time I saw Russell was in the small private departure lounge at Hatfield, where he was positioning up on one of the company shuttles to Prestwick. Politely folding his newspaper as we exchanged a few pleasantries he was, as always, calm and polite.

On 6th October 1992, barely feet above the runway at Prestwick whilst undergoing an engine failure simulation in a real aeroplane over real concrete, the aircraft impacted the ground with such violence that, after the ensuing fireball, all that remained recognisable was the tail sticking out with the aircraft registration.

I did not know the captain, but the impact on me with the loss of Russell was great, and my feeling that of complete and utter disbelief.

After the coroner's report had concluded, the *Glasgow Herald* reported:

> 'Sheriff Gow said that changes in the law and in the rules of air navigation are best made by Parliament on the recommendation of the CAA.

The pilots who died [...] were engaged in a simulated engine failure test when their plane crashed 16 seconds after take-off on October 6, 1992. Sheriff Gow said: "The evidence was such that emergencies are extremely rare in practice and that accidents are, in fact, reported more frequently in simulated conditions than in real conditions."

If these tests were carried out at sufficient height, then the pilots would have enough time to recover from any mistakes, he suggested. Turning to the suggestion that engine failure tests might be transferred to ground-based simulators instead of flying tests in potentially hazardous situations, the Sheriff noted that in the US -- where the majority of 300 exported Jetstreams are based -- there are five or six simulators.

Noting that "an extremely extensive and expensive" investigation had been carried out by the AAIB (Air Accident Investigation Branch) with the full co-operation of Jetstream Limited, he said he was satisfied that every possible step had been taken to find with reasonable certainty the causes of the accident.

Sheriff Gow said the interests of the families had been "very adequately represented."

https://www.heraldscotland.com/news/12695211.
prestwick-air-crash-a-tragic-accident/

After I had left British Aerospace, one of the pilots I had flown with was tragically killed in an accident at Dunsfold Aerodrome in Surrey following an engine failure/fire in a Hawker Hunter when he was thrown from the aircraft following impact.

The AAIB report is extensive, but in essence, due to the massive disruption to the structure at the first impact, the ejector seat became inoperative with a series of events resulting as follows:

'As the aircraft had bounced and cart wheeled across the runway, the unrestrained pilot had probably been thrown out of the right side of the cockpit wreckage and then dragged by the main parachute canopy withdrawal line which had failed to release from the ejection seat headbox. During this process the parachute ripcord pins had pulled out, and the main parachute canopy and rigging lines had been pulled from the parachute packing case. The pilot's personal survival pack (PSP) had also torn open and the life raft released from its container.'

https://assets.publishing.service.gov.uk/media/5422f5f0ed915d1374000589/dft_avsafety_pdf_502233.pdf

In World War II, there were reputedly more pilots killed in flying accidents and training accidents in the Mosquito twin engine fighter/bomber than in combat. The Mosquito, which I had been so fortunate to fly in, crashed at Barton near Manchester in 1996 with two other Bae pilots.

RR299 had been operated by British Aerospace from Hawarden since the early 1960s. The aircraft had come to the end of its display sequence when, during the final wing over, a manoeuvre which involves the aircraft reversing its course by climbing and rolling to the left or right, the left engine lost power and the subsequent control loss and attempted recovery resulted in the aircraft crashing into woods and bog, killing both crew. The engines were buried so deep excavators were needed for wreckage recovery. Recommendations were made as a result of this accident in relation to the carburettors and servicing of Rolls Royce Merlin-powered aircraft.

A pivotal moment for me with respect to fate taking a hand in events was when I had the opportunity to fly with the Royal Air Force in a Hawk Jet Trainer at RAF Valley in Anglesey, North Wales. At this stage of my career I was flying long-haul, back in an airline environment. An exchange programme had been operating for a while where we would take an RAF pilot on a trip with the airline, and they would reciprocate. In my case, I was paired up with a RAF Flt Lt.

It so happened that I was scheduled to start a command course, transitioning to captain at the same time. However, I was moving from the Airbus A340 as a first officer to the A320 as a captain, which was great for me but not for my RAF partner! The reason being that the A340 went to the sexy long-haul destinations, and the only A320 we operated shuttled back and forwards between London Heathrow, Athens and London Gatwick. (Not that Athens is not sexy!) So we hatched a plan and set off for Hong Kong, taking my RAF exchange partner along for the ride before I changed fleets.

It was my thirty-ninth Hong Kong trip to Kai Tak, and it was also to be my last for a while, so the plan was to enjoy it! Upon our return to the UK, we were scheduled to land back at Heathrow on the Sunday, and I would travel up on the Monday to RAF Valley by train; and, regardless of the weather, we would fly the 'weather ship', a Hawk that went out to check the low flying routes and weather in the training areas at the beginning of the day's activities. That was the plan . . . except on the way home I had a severe case of what is technically known as 'the trots', or in medical terms diarrhoea, from suspected food poisoning. It was agreed that an additional twenty-four hours rest would be a sensible idea before strapping into a Hawk.

My RAF exchange partner made the necessary arrangements, and the day I was originally supposed to fly the Hawk with him (the weather ship), I set off on the train up to London, Victoria, the intention being to then fly the following day instead.

London was on an extremely heightened state of security as the IRA had resumed their bombing campaign and struck the Docklands financial district on the Friday before. On the Sunday, the day we landed back at Heathrow from Hong Kong, the UK government had increased their security warnings to the extent that they said a bombing could take place 'anywhere and at any time' in the UK.

So it was with trepidation I crossed London, using the Underground, and with caution I came up the escalators into Kings Cross. As I walked across the concourse, over the Tannoy I heard my name: 'Would [...] please report immediately to British Transport Police for an urgent message.' Surely not?

The station was awash with uniformed officers after the IRA bombing, and I stepped forward and identified myself, at which point I was literally marched across to the British Transport Police office, where an officer said, "You are to phone RAF Valley immediately, sir!"

I called the number I had previously been given and was told they could not explain anything right now, but I was to turn around immediately and get back home then, once home, call back. Which I promised I would, convinced that the base was on lock down. It had to be a security incident.

When I got home I called . . . and was told the devastating news that the weather ship we had originally been scheduled to fly that morning had crashed on takeoff, killing the pilot.

The press were later to report:

'The initial RAF accident bulletin indicates that the Hawk's ailerons were disconnected. The RAF declines to comment.

The aircraft had been taken off the flight line for non-destructive testing, at which point the ailerons were disconnected. Part of the investigation is focusing on concerns over the documentation covering the work of the aircraft. The Hawk has hydro-mechanical controls, with the exception of the rudder, which is mechanical.

The ailerons should have been reconnected before the aircraft was returned to the flight line. As part of the pre-flight checks, correct control-surface input and movement should also have been visually confirmed by the pilot and ground crew. The pilot would have been unable to tell from stick feel that the ailerons were disconnected. The bulletin re-stressed that aircrew must make sure that all control surfaces move correctly as part of the pre-flight checks.

The aircraft began to roll shortly after take-off. The pilot is believed to have ejected at low level as the aircraft rolled beyond 90° and was killed.' (flightglobal.com)

https://www.flightglobal.com/news/articles/
disconnected-ailerons-are-blamed-for-raf-hawk-
crash-17706/

The pilot had been a veteran of the Gulf War and had survived an ejection in combat, which was followed by six weeks in captivity. A lot of my colleagues in the airline knew him well and he was well respected.

The impact of the tragedy on everyone was profound, and the ripples of those touched by it stretched a long way. I was later told, though I do not know if it was true, that an engineer involved had subsequently taken his life. If true, then my thoughts are with his family also.

Within the airline, the managers who organised the military exchanges went into panic mode as questions were asked about 'risk', 'liability' and 'legal' ramifications if I, or any airline pilot, was killed participating in such a high-risk endeavour. Fortunately, our chief pilot at the time, and all of the flight operations management, were consummate professionals and pragmatic. I was invited to the office to share what I thought, and to ask any questions I had.

For me it was obvious: we continue with the exchanges because, as has always been the case, they are purely on a voluntary basis. As pilots we understand risk; but we also understand how to mitigate risk as best we can, and that if life is worth living, it is also worth experiencing.

But I was conscious that if too long a gap was left before the next exchange flight, the nay-sayers would become more and more vocal, and before we knew it the programme would be binned. I shared my thoughts with the RAF exchange pilot, and within weeks I was strapped into XX173 flying out of RAF Valley straight into the low level route of North Wales.

Pulling G was not something I had a lot of experience of, and whilst turns were around 4G, which is not a lot for fighter pilots, for a BUS driver it was! I had been given the controls early into the flight and after 're-educating' me on how to turn a high-performance jet which is basically on its side pulling G, I had a blast. I remember seeing a red Post Office van above us on the A5 as we hurtled down a valley!

Part of our pre-flight briefing was to conduct a simulated low-level attack on the flight test portacabin on 2 Site at Hawarden, where I knew Agnes, PA to the Bae test pilots, would probably be putting the kettle on. The run in and attack was pre-arranged with the airfield, but I had neglected to forewarn Agnes, who subsequently shared her 'explicit' thoughts on the matter when I called to find out if the teapot was still intact.

Following the railway line on the north of the airfield by the canal, we stormed west back to Anglesey, where some aerobatics and circuits completed the flight. I was physically and mentally exhausted, and as we taxied into the dispersal area following our sortie I could feel my gyros starting to topple and, as the canopy opened and the fresh air hit me, I reached for the sick bag in my flying suit and promptly filled it!

Afterwards I was re-assured I was not a complete 'wuss', as it was not unusual for people to be ill after a flight once the sensory overload was turned off and you were back on the ground; but from the photograph afterwards you can see clearly I am made of 'the wrong stuff"!

Without doubt, going ahead with the flight in the wake of such an awful tragedy was important, not from a personal perspective but for the squadron that hosted me: it allowed them to keep moving forward.

It is not just high performance aircraft that can be involved in tragedy, however, and risk is present in any form of flight, including gliders, microlights, light aircraft and hot air balloons. Anything that flies basically. The trick is to manage the risk as much as possible.

I have always had an interest in light aircraft, and coupled with my engineering background it was only natural that I would someday own my own. I found what, for me, was the perfect candidate and bought a C23 Beech Sundowner, which is built like a battleship and was indeed used, I believe, by the Canadian Air Force as a primary trainer for a while.

Like all Beechcraft products it was over-engineered and robust. Just what I needed! And I knew this particular aircraft was strong, as I discovered that in its previous life it featured in an incident report for carrying a concrete tie down block around the circuit. Fortunately it was spotted by the tower on takeoff, and the subsequent landing resulted in damage only to the runway, and presumably much embarrassment.

I took the aircraft to Coventry and we set about a major annual inspection, at the end of which she was stripped and painted in a scheme I had used before on a Beech Baron. She was a joy to fly, and being fixed gear and fixed prop was simple to operate and maintain.

It was a summer's day in 2011; one of those days when aircraft are meant to be flown and pilots are meant to fly. Visibility was estimated to be in excess of thirty miles, and the South of England glowed in the warmth of the summer sun, with the English Channel shimmering as if airbrushed in to add a frame to the island upon which it lapped. It was too good an opportunity to miss, and I took my son down to Shoreham-by-Sea and pulled out the Sundowner so we could enjoy the day and fly.

The flight was a joy, and we flew out to the west to Selsey, a large prominent spit of land passing the former World War II airfields HMS Peregrine (Ford Aerodrome) and Tangmere[15]. Returning to Shoreham, we joined the circuit flying downwind towards the Downs, rising in front and then a base leg over the escarpment to the River Adur and finals for runway 20. Parking on the apron in front of the hangar on the southern side of the airfield, not far from the runway, we climbed out on either side and stood there basking in the beauty of the stunning day, having just concluded a memorable flight.

I heard a shout go up, and swung around, catching site of a black mushroom cloud rising from the area to the east outside of the airfield boundary towards the river estuary. My heart sank when I saw people running out of hangars. I then heard a whooshing rattle to my left, on the grass runway and central grass area of the middle of the airfield. No engine noise, just the sound of motion: curving towards us was a low wing aeroplane with the front smashed and wisps of smoke. The noise stopped, followed immediately by

---

[15] As an aside, the houses encroaching onto Tangmere were visibly stripping it of its dignity as a former Battle of Britain airfield and former home, not only to Lysander SOE night flights supporting resistance in occupied Europe, but post-war from where Neville Duke set the record in a Hunter as part of the high speed flight trials.

the sound of the airfield fire engine heading away and out of the airfield.

I ran with my son, straight out to this crippled aeroplane, and was the first to reach it. I had already built a picture of what was going on around me, and knew immediately there had been a mid-air collision.

In front of me was a Diamond low wing training aircraft from one of the airfield flying schools, with extensive damage to the front and the propeller missing. The left-hand wing had sustained extensive damage, too, and the pilot had successfully made a dead stick landing with no power.

But I had no idea what I would find when I saw the two occupants. I swung around to my son and screamed "STOP!" My fear was that both of the pilots were severely injured, and I needed to face this on my own.

Simultaneously, both pilots – who it transpired later were instructors – got out without a mark on them. One of them, the younger one, started walking off across the airfield. An engineer from the hangars raced after him. The older instructor stood in front of me and just stared, in complete and utter shock.

I said, "Is the battery isolated? Is the master switch off?"

Nothing.

I shouted at him: "*Is the battery isolated? Is the master switch off?*"

He muttered something incoherent, and went back to the aircraft. He appeared to turn something off in the cockpit.

Then we just stood there on our own, with no airport vehicles, in disbelief. I asked one of the engineers where the fire engine was, and he confirmed it had gone to the aircraft that had crashed off the airfield. I suggested we grab a fire extinguisher from the hangar and get everyone well clear, as the left wing damage was so severe I had no idea if there was a fuel cell ruptured. We made our way back to the hangar and airport staff came over a short while afterwards.

The other aircraft had crashed in a small park area off of the airfield, and despite the heroic attempts of an off duty policeman, the fire was too intense. (It was surmised as part of the coroner's report that the impact had proven to be fatal prior to the subsequent fire.) It had lost significant sections of its tail feathers, rendering the aircraft un controllable after the Diamond had impacted the tail within the airfield circuit.

Out of respect to all of those involved and their families, this is not the place to review the accident in detail. However, it had a significant impact on me, and made me question myself pursuing an interest that was purely for self-gratification. My son was sixteen at the time . . . what right did I have to subject him to risk on this level? Not logical you might say, as life is full of risks. But it made me stop and think.

The first thing I did was accept that I too could miss seeing other aircraft. Whilst in an airliner, I had sophisticated traffic collision avoidance systems; in the Sundowner I did not. The first thing I did before I flew again was buy a system and have it installed. The cost was irrelevant.

Again, this is not the platform to look at the accident report in detail, but there was a section on electronic traffic detection devices that vindicated my immediate reaction of installing a system. The AAIB report included references to alerting systems, and since 2011 there has been a significant increase in their use. Some light aircraft manufacturers even include it now as standard equipment.

The following is from the report:

'Numerous limitations, including those of the human visual system, the demands of cockpit tasks, and various physical and environmental conditions combine to make see-and-avoid an uncertain method of traffic separation' (Limitations of the See-and-Avoid Principle; ATSB Research Report, April 1991.

Studies in 1991 showed that alerted see-and-avoid is eight times more effective than unalerted. There is no requirement for traffic alerting systems to be fitted to light aircraft.

Both GC and ZR were operating Mode S transponders and both were equipped with EFIS displays that could have been fitted with a traffic alerting system. Stand-alone alerting systems were also available. (Unalerted Air to Air Visual Acquisition, J W Andrews, November 1991, Massachusetts Institute of Technology.)'

https://assets.publishing.service.gov.uk/
media/5422ec3340f0b613460000e3/Vans_RV-
6A_G-RVGC_and_DA_40D_Diamond_Star_G-
CEZR_06-12.pdf

Line flying brings with it risk, and on two occasions I had a requirement to reject a takeoff on public transport flights, with passengers and crew depending on us to get it right. On both occasions they were at around 80 knots; and on both occasions there was absolutely no ambiguity as to whether the takeoff should or should not be abandoned.

The first occasion was not long after getting my command on the A320. We were departing Heathrow on 27R, and due to a nose wheel steering fault an un-commanded left turn was fed into the nose wheel actuators and the aircraft literally tried to exit stage left! The interesting thing for me was that the amount of right rudder I had to put in was so great and so quick with a yaw to the left that my instinct was that it was an engine failure, and I just shouted "Stop!" and executed the rejected takeoff. It was only after we had stopped did the warning pages flash up on the screen directing us towards a steering fault.

The second occasion was later in my career on a B747-200 in the Caribbean, and we had, if I remember correctly, a 'red master' warning, a 'wheel well fire' warning, and a 'gear unsafe' indication, which again was an easy decision: "Stop." As we rocked to a stop, I recall swinging around to the flight engineer and saying, "Is there still a fire indication?" to which he responded "No."

This second incident was a lot easier to manage, as we had three flight deck crew, which included a flight engineer. The flight engineer quickly ascertained that all of the landing gear were exactly where they were supposed to be and that we were not on fire. It turned out to be a spurious fault generated by the warning systems.

The first officer had, in addition to monitoring all of our actions and confirming them, been able to manage ATC, who wanted us to vacate immediately due to another aircraft approaching to land. However, we were not going to move until we were absolutely sure we were in a safe condition to do so.

I, in the meantime, had made a passenger address to calm everyone down and had briefed the cabin crew via the flight service manager.

Both of these incidents were dealt with exactly as they would have been if any other line pilot had been in that position, and was simply down to training. You practice rejected takeoffs over and over again during the course of your career. Some people never ever have to put the training into practice. It just so happens I had two!

Indeed, flying is complex and not without risk.

But is the risk disproportionate to other human activities? Driving, for example? No.

Has any of this stopped me from flying, or enjoying the freedom and benefits? No.

What is important is understanding the cause and effect of all of our actions, particularly in an aeroplane.

Chapter 12

Flying the Line

A tried and tested route across the North Atlantic, from Newfoundland to the southern tip of Greenland and across to Iceland. Then onward to the Scottish Highlands, Prestwick, and then to the South to England. A route flown by DC-3s, B17s, and countless ferry pilots for over half a century of aircraft being delivered to Europe from the United States in times of peace and times of war.

It may come as a surprise to learn that in the early 1990s, a slow flow of aircraft in the opposite direction took place. These aircraft left the factory at Hawarden near Chester, and went to various completion centres in the United States. The venerable 125 was a remarkable success story.

They first saw the grey of day (as anybody who has spent time in the northwest of England will agree) on flight test, climbing out towards Wrexham, very quickly turning away, raking their nose across the peaks of Snowdon, banking across Wales and out into the open Irish Sea. Climbing, rising and falling. Tested above the trawlers, ferries and bulbous silhouettes below the surface at periscope depth, trailing wash, scarring the sea; tested with care and tested for life. And breathing for the first time the Atlantic air rolling across Ireland.

'Off test': the magic words written at the bottom of the pilot's final flight test report; a release into service; a release from birth in the Cheshire plain to the world beyond.

Some aircraft were completed with mahogany, teak and fine English leather by the craftsmen and women of Chester. Dressed to dazzle and shine, covet, caress and seduce their charge.

Others started their lives as aluminium shells, stripped of interior, glass cockpits, autopilots and yaw dampers. Coming 'off test' without a gown, naked, inhibited yet aggressive in their stance. Rivets in rows shoulder to shoulder in green primer, resembling an aircraft destined for combat rather than the luxury of Paris's Le Bourget.

As always, looks can be deceiving, for the ugly ducklings were destined to be dressed in Arkansas, Delaware, Texas and Kansas.

It all started with the words 'off test', the message conveyed to Hatfield, the airfield founded by Sir Geoffrey de Havilland, and where a ferry crew would be notified. Lawyers prepared contracts and planning commenced.

A good hot English breakfast is mandatory. I don't normally eat such a large breakfast, relying on cereal to hold me through until lunch time. But this day I found myself looking out across the Cheshire regiment's barracks, the slate grey glistening as the rain swept across the city.

The International is, without doubt, a comfortable hotel set within the heart of the Roman walled city of Chester. It prepares me well. The scrambled eggs and bacon create a pulse of condensation against the window. Across the table sits my companion for the journey ahead. His face is furrowed with creases from time spent in the tropics. His skin is leathered and his hair, though grey, still has its waves, as it did thirty years ago when blond. He barks with strength, as if delivering a line of Shakespeare. Indeed he could, with little encouragement, step into *Henry V* and deliver, 'Once more unto the breach. . .' with eyes of steel.

He doesn't say a lot, and it is normal to find occasional sentences interspersed with long minutes of sipping of tea.

But then, "Bloody good start!" he spurts, glaring at the rain as it fans across the roof of the barracks. The grey mass overhead reaches down in fingers trailing across the city; dark streaks of tentacles snaking over the chimney pots and gables, beating down in a continues torrent.

"Just like Keflavik," I reply. "Preparing us for it."

"Bloody typical. First ferry flight I get in a couple of months and it's like a typhoon out there!"

I finish off the toast; I have to eat it all as I am going to call upon it later to provide me with warmth from within. I can feel a bead of sweat on the inside of my calf. I shouldn't have put the thermal leggings on so soon, even though it made sense at the time. (Just the fisherman's socks and the thick NATO sweater with its padded shoulders to go.)

"Ten minutes," he says, and is up and gone, back to his room and checked out.

Dashing from the elevator to the car park on the hotel roof, we throw our bags into the back of the car. At full speed, the wipers cannot cope and brake lights cascade across the film of water. After a brief journey, out of the spray comes the whiteboard: 'Free Range Eggs'. This is the only indication of a driveway, leading to the entrance of 2 Site, where Wellington bombers were once assembled. You could be forgiven for believing that they still are, for this part of the airfield has not changed at all since those days in the early 1940s.

On the perimeter track we drive past blister hangars, fighter pens, workshops, air raid shelters and the relics of war, in some places replaced with red, white and blue covering the camouflage paint. It shows no sign of investment. On the far side, Airbus have purpose-built hangars and show advancement with technology; but on 2 Site, the corporate jet operation resembles a living dinosaur.

We round the corporate jet hangar, with its semi-circular roof and external steel support, to see our aircraft, engines running. Engineers are scurrying around, performing the last checks, and yellow raincoats are the order of the day, for rain is unrelenting, driving across the airfield, the grass rippling and fanning out as the pulses hit. A stream pours off one corner of the flight test building, bouncing off the concrete back towards the roof.

An umbilical cord of power trails from the aircraft to a ground power unit. The generator groans, with black smoke belching out every thirty seconds, which sweeps past the fuselage before rising away on the merciless wind.

The green portacabin sits in between the railway line and the hangar, shuddering as a locomotive pulling coal from the mines to the power station at Liverpool thunders by. Too close. Inside the portacabin an office has a table covered with manuals and papers. I turn into the office opposite, that serves as a flight operations room, and pull the weather and flight plan off the fax machine. The other pilot is working through the aircraft documentation with a quality inspector, ticking off an inventory list.

Customs arrive and, on cue, Agnes appears with a pot of tea. As the flight test secretary, Agnes has a permanent grin as she chaperones her boys in the flight test department, and is the source of all information, fact or fiction, and able to inject a wicked giggle in between sentences, thus managing what is a serious business with humour.

From within the bowels of the portacabins, a chant is heard from a pipe. Gaelic in origin, haunting tunes fill the air as the weather crashes into the side of the cabin. The chief test pilot has his door closed and practices his pipe music.

I review the weather forecasts and current actual. Keflavik in Iceland is reporting westerly winds at 25 knots, gusting to 40 knots, 800 feet overcast, and rain mixed with ice pellets up to 14,000 feet.

Sondrestrom in Greenland, too far north to be of practical use but an escape route if needed, is clear, and Narssasarak in the south, over which we will fly, no report.

Goose, Gander, Bangor, Boston and Montreal all okay, with the lowest actual quarter mile in fog, with forecasts all showing to be better than CAT I minima for the estimated time of arrival.

Notices to Airman show the Glasgow VOR beacon as being off the air – not a problem as we will swing up to Stornaway before heading out.

The tea is refreshing as we sit to reflect and collect our thoughts before going out to the aircraft. The senior captain, Chris, signs for the aircraft documents and we review the technical log book.

"I'll do the walk around," I call.

Chris grins at me in gratitude, knowing I will get soaked despite wet weather gear. "I'll load up and get everything set up, then. You kick off, seeing as you're getting wet! Might as well get something out of it," he says, still grinning.

I'm happy, as it means I get to fly to Iceland, and that is always a challenge; plus, with three sectors, it means I will probably be flying two out of three. Worth getting soaked for.

The aircraft is a 1000 series Bae 125 'greenie', devoid of finished paint and covered in etch primer; just a skeleton of structure. Without a doubt, the 1000 is by far better looking compared to the 800, with better proportions and, I felt, better handling, feeling more solid and powerful with its big Pratt & Whitney Canada 305 engines on their respective rear mounts.

With the bags onboard, I lean forward into the cockpit, visually checking the gear down, locked indicators, hydraulic indicators and battery conditions on the electrical panel. Flash light in hand, I start the external pre-flight inspection.

Onboard, I peer through the rain to make one last check that there is nothing in front of the aircraft, swing the door closed and push the handle down, locking it securely. Stripping off my wet jacket I hang it on a bare green fuselage frame, able to hook the plastic hangar on a lightening hole.

The thermal space blanket hangs limp just behind the entrance way, separating the entire cabin from the front section of the aircraft. Pulling the curtain to one side, I look back and see the boxes of manuals, along with spares, all lashed to the floor. Food boxes of sandwiches and fruit sit jammed in between, along with flasks of coffee. The single hot air bleed duct runs forward into our front section, giving us a degree of comfort, but not enough to discard the extra layers.

We quickly get started and sit patiently as the single VLF Omega and portable navigation unit is programmed with the requisite waypoints. The ferry kit is basic. We lack modern GPS or backup systems. Then, without any fanfares or salutes, a simple thumbs-up from the ground crew indicates we are clear to taxi out with a brand-new aircraft and five hours total time in the tech log.

Hawarden's runway is not long enough for us to comfortably carry enough fuel to get to Goose Bay in Labrador, so we head for Keflavik where, having filled up, we will continue to Bangor, Maine, hopefully the same day.

We are in good shape for getting to Bangor in daylight, and with the thrust levers in the takeoff gate we surge down the runway. With my hand firmly on the rams horns that are used for the control yoke, I rotate and we climb straight into the soup, instantly losing site of the ground. The turbulence off the hills and mountains to the west jar the little business jet as I turn right, swinging all the way around to head north. As we climb higher, the first indications of potential ice initiates our use of the TKS, and fluid seeps out of the tiny holes in the leading edges – a crude but effective system.

With no autopilot and no yaw damper, I physically feel each jolt and pitch change as we climb ever higher and break out in the clear, passing 26,000 feet. You get to learn very quickly the effects of control inputs, and the higher you fly the more sensitive the aircraft is to every touch. You learn to trim accurately, too, as it helps with turbulence, allowing the aircraft to return to its original attitude with the smallest of corrections. You learn to be at one with the aircraft.

The stop at Keflavik is uneventful and, after refuelling, with Chris now in the left seat, we head for OZN Prince Christian on the southern tip of Greenland. I work the HF with Iceland and switch to Gander as we cross 30 west. Ahead I can see the glaciers clearly on the eastern side and, as predicted by the met office, we start picking up some standing waves caused by Greenland forcing the air to porpoise over its mountains. Chris allows the aircraft to ride the waves plus or minus 100 feet from our assigned altitude, and not once does he trigger an altitude alert indicating we have deviated more than 250 feet.

It sounds easy, but it's not. Hand flying a jet at altitude is tiring and, when necessary, we hand over control to each other and stretch our wrists and hands, jumping up for a sandwich and coffee. I marvel at the ice forming behind us on the inside of the bare cabin.

Switching to Gander centre, we are identified coasting in and cleared through Moncton's airspace to Bangor. On the radio I recognize the distinctive voice of a pilot I knew several years earlier when we were flying B737s in the holiday charter world. Now he plies his trade in a B747.

As we line up on the ILS at Bangor, I can clearly see the runway stretching out in front of us. It is enormous compared to our humble Hawarden nestled in the Welsh borders. Bangor is a B52 and KC-135 base with an Air National Guard unit on the airfield as well. The runway appears to be as wide as it is long and literally swallows us whole.

On the ramp we are met by US Immigration and Customs, along with 'Derringer', who are our agents, importing the aircraft into the United States.

I like Bangor.

We stay in the airport Hilton and in the bar have a clear view of the runway and are able to satisfy any closet 'aviation enthusiast' tendencies either of us have; but we quickly move downstairs to grab a taxi to Captain Nick`s to gorge on seafood. Why not?

The next morning after the aircraft is confirmed as cleared by customs, we walk the short distance to the flight service station, located adjacent to the ramp. These stations in the States are invaluable in their ability to provide weather and notam information for any pilot, private or commercial. With our flight plan filed for the last leg down to Little Rock, Arkansas, we head out.

By lunchtime we find ourselves parked outside the completion centre handing over a brand new Hawker 1000. The aircraft will spend several months having its avionics and interior fitted exactly as specified by the customer. And within a couple of hours we are on an American Airlines commuter flying to Dallas Fort Worth for the connection back to Gatwick. We will be back in the UK less than forty-eight hours after leaving Hawarden.

oOo

'Self-loading freight' is a derogatory expression. Used by some to describe their human charges. Used as a shield in order to divorce accountability in numbers. The young, the old and the in between. Whether ten or 500, they are still people, still self-loading. And whether loved or unloved, in a rainbow of race and creeds they inhale and exhale the same volume of air every two and a half seconds.

Regardless of the volume or capacity behind the pilot's seats, mortal or material, the aircraft will still travel through time and space, requiring the same attention given to heading changes, rate of climb and thrust changes.

At London Heathrow, the faces can be seen against the glass, impatient and anxious to board lest we close the doors, empty, and push back away from the terminal, cheating them of their journey. The floor is scattered with children, cross-legged, waiting.

From the cockpit at eye level the plastic bags of duty free can be seen clutched with pride. The child at knee-height continually points past your line of site, first at the baggage being fed on a conveyor belt into the bowels of the aeroplane, then at a bigger brighter aircraft that has taxied behind.

Then blue stone-washed jeans and a black t-shirt, blonde short cropped hair, an earring and a stomach, the years of beer-drinking carried as a trophy out in front. Duty free bags are in one hand, the *Racing Times* in the other.

Silhouettes move past in the distance, beginning to blur as the pressure builds around the entrance to the jet bridge. A bottleneck has formed and will not be relieved until the boarding has completed.

The cabin crewmember at the boarding door smiles, and her pearl earrings glisten as a shaft of light through the jet bridge service door bounces across, then stop shining as the clouds tighten their noose on the airport, shutting off the gap and shutting off the light. Her smile is consistent.

The cockpit speaker chatters with rhetoric.

The cabin speaker is muffled and unintelligible, until the cockpit door opens and in steps the turnaround coordinator, sometimes referred to as a 'red cap' from decades before, when that was what they wore. "Captain, one LMC," he says, and hands me the amended load sheet with the last minute change.

I advise him of the airfield delays and our need to get in the queue. The TCO glances at his watch and turns on his heels, knowing five minutes is all he has.

The four hundredth and fifty-sixth passenger crosses the threshold onto the aircraft, and with a quick acknowledgement of the headcount, I ask for the door to be closed. I can see the holds are closed. No time for a PA, and we are onto Air Traffic to join the queue for pushback. Fifteen minutes airfield delay. That will make us nine minutes late on pushback. Okay . . . time for a PA.

"Ladies and gentlemen . . ."

With the 'before start' checklist completed we are cleared to push and start. I can see in the reflection of the terminal glass the tug is connected and the ground engineer is clear of the tow bar. Good.

With an exchange between the two of us via his headset, I release the parking brake. The B747's nose gently dips in salute as it is pulled forward a foot and stops, the chocks being pulled clear, the big lumbering aeroplane rocks back, as we begin to push away from the gate.

Starting the engines in turn, the 'after start' checks are completed and the tug sits over to my left, clear of the double white line, out of harm's way. The engineer walks away, not turning but facing away, waiting. When he is beside the tug he turns and holds up the pin that was in our nose gear, isolating hydraulics from the steering mechanism. With the pin clear, and all the ground equipment clear, we call for taxi clearance.

Slowly I walk the thrust levers up, ever so slightly, and wait for a response. The aircraft starts to move.

The flight is uneventful. I always enjoy flying with James, something I think about as we cross the Atlantic towards Boston.

The constant chatter on the radio with Boston Approach fires heading and altitude changes at us as I bring the 747 around the corner onto the localizer, just slightly below the glideslope in anticipation of its capture.

As we fly down, the ILS fully configured, I can feel every ripple through the airframe as we cross the threshold to 22L, the sea lapping the airport as it floats, as if suspended in the harbour. The city to my right stretches up, giving the illusion of mountainous terrain. My right hand is ever so gently moving the thrust levers, maintaining the target speed as the radar altimeter calls out our height over the asphalt.

The back of the big bogies hanging off the four main undercarriages rumble onto the runway, the vibration slightly running up through the aeroplane to my fingers and toes on the rudder pedals.

The speed brakes deploy and, as the nose wheel is flown onto the runway, I crack the thrust reversers and, when deployed, we decelerate as if in slow motion. I lose all sense of speed being sat so high on top of this technological marvel produced by Boeing in Seattle.

We have arrived. It is early evening, 10th September 2001.

The following day would become infamous as the events of September 11th unfolded around us.

Pilots are creatures of habit, and for as long as I can remember we have always been to the same diner for breakfast of steak and eggs sat atop a sea of hash browns, and then proceeded to the Mall. To spend an hour or two before driving back in the flight deck car, which was a pool car we all contributed to on the fleet, with a chance to relax before trying to sleep for a couple of hours in the early afternoon, checkout, airport, and then fly through the night home.

This, for us, was no different to any other night stop Boston.

The hotel is sat on a hill at Danvers, just outside of Boston in a country club, and is rumoured to have been built as a hospital, as the corridors and doors are extremely wide. The crew called it 'The Shining Hotel' after the Jack Nicholson horror film, as some swore they had seen a child riding a tricycle up and down the corridors at night!

James and I, full of steak and eggs, once inside the shopping mall, agree what time to meet back up and go our separate ways. I go straight downstairs in Sears, to where all of the tools are, as I want some bits and pieces.

As I walk towards the tool section through the electrical area, I can see a whole bunch of people stood around the televisions shaking their heads . . . but there is complete silence. As I approach, on the screen I can clearly see the Twin Towers in New York. One of them is belching flames and smoke out of a cavernous hole in the side.

"Terrorists," I say to the person next to me, knowing they have been targeted before.

"Looks like it," he replies.

I carry on. It has not hit me at all what is actually going on, and my assumption is simply that it was a bomb. I decide, however, to find James, and head upstairs to the main concourse and, straightaway, James, who had spotted me, walks briskly towards me.

"Have you seen what has happened?" he asks.

"Yeah, it looks like someone has let one off in the World Trade Centre."

"No," he replies. "An aeroplane has been flown into it."

"Shit."

It's time to get back to the hotel.

As we drive that morning, on a crisp and stunningly beautiful day with not a cloud in the sky, we tune into the radio. It was completely surreal. It was as if we were listening to Orson Welles reading the 'The War of the Worlds'. Yet the commentator delivered the news in a calm, factual way, as if narrating a scene being played out on a stage.

Back at the hotel, as we enter the lobby, I ask the front desk and concierge to stop any crewmembers from leaving the hotel and to get a message to all of them to meet urgently in the crew room. James and I then manage to get together with the flight service manager and, with all of the crew waiting in the crew room, I walk in to see a lot of them in tears as they watch the devastation unfold before us live on television.

I know it is up to us to make rapid decisions, as we do not know if we are watching an isolated event (comparatively), or a global event, and other things are happening. Through the station manager at Boston we get an open landline to our operations department, and I am able to talk to our chief pilot.

James and I decide to use the 'lifeboat drill', which is basically what you do when the ship has sunk in the middle of the Atlantic, leaving you responsible for a handful of survivors in a lifeboat. Right up there with shelter and food is the mental ability and willingness to survive . . . and not dwell on what has just happened. The way you do this is by assigning everybody a task, or 'purpose'.

So the first thing we do is task some of the crew with going out in a van to Costco to buy supplies, as we have no idea what our next move would be.

I had already discussed a contingency plan with our operations department of getting a coach to run us north and into Canada, away from Boston if necessary, as at that moment in time, chemical weapons or 'dirty bombs' were still perceived as a threat. Our logic was simply to get the crew out of harm's way, and with two of the hijacked aircraft having originated out of Boston, we had to think of options. Flying out was not an option.

The station manager and the staff at Boston were embroiled in the total shutdown of the airport and SWAT teams were running around along with the FBI. This, as you can imagine, was being played out across the United States with crews across the network, and we were safe compared to the horrific challenges in New York with crew at the time unaccounted for. The way the crew I was responsible for conducted themselves was exemplary, and they supported me in a way that I will forever be in gratitude for.

Because Boston was a crime scene, it was, along with Washington National Airport, one of the last to re-open, and it was not until the very early hours of 17th September that we took off from Logan to fly home, operating the first company flight out of Logan Airport.

Having been cleared for takeoff, with the city of Boston lit up in front of us, James brought the thrust levers up together and the nose gently bobbed up as the thrust bit into the night air.

Over the radio the Tower controller said, "Godspeed, Virgin."

Chapter 13

Challenge and Reward

There are a myriad of situations you can be faced with as a line pilot. It helps if you can understand what the challenges are likely to be, all the way from technical issues to personality issues, and learn to diffuse potentially difficult situations. It also helps to understand that everybody has a job to do.

We were getting ready to pushback one night from London Heathrow on our way to Hong Kong. The first officer was new to the company, new to the aircraft, and new to the civilian environment having just left the military. Ninety-nine times out of a 100, the new pilots, especially ex-military, are extremely competent and polite, and take their time to absorb a new environment. Then there is the one in 100 who don't.

The first officer was flying the first sector to Hong Kong and was ricocheting around like a fire cracker, rushing everyone, the consequence being that he was getting everyone's back up. I knew that in order to ensure that over the next twelve hours we were fed and watered, and avoided any unnecessary drama, we all needed to get on. I needed to intervene.

The line engineer came onto the flight deck and was just about to talk to me when the first officer swung around and barked an order at him. The engineer was dripping wet, with his high-vis coat shimmering under the yellow dome light like a seal pup covered in oil and hydraulic fluid. I watched him turn his entire body around, his chest rising as he drew large volumes of air deep into his lungs.

I stretched out my hand and said to the first officer, "Look, we can discuss this later, but right now he needs to do his job and talk directly to me. Can you grab the latest weather while I wrap up the tech log please?"

It worked.

The engineer swung back towards me and gave me a knowing grin, as we both knew he was a millisecond from ripping into the first officer.

To give the new guy credit, he apologized later for stepping on my toes. I explained that that was not the issue, but it was the way he had barked orders at the engineer. It was simply not acceptable.

Engineers. You have to respect them; after all, you depend on them.

Flying the line as a ferry pilot is completely different to flying the line as an airline pilot or corporate pilot. There are, however, common experiences that relate to all, and any pilot will agree that the biggest threat is undoubtedly fatigue and jet lag.

Countless reams have been written by medical experts, aviation specialists, regulatory authorities and flight operations departments about jet lag, crew rest and fatigue; and as a pilot, I and thousands of my colleagues will testify it is the most debilitating and unpleasant thing you can possibly experience. Passengers can testify to the effect after an Atlantic crossing; but try doing it again twenty-four hours later, and then forty-eight hours after that. That is not five, but eight hour time zones. And another forty-eight hours later, you have to go back in the opposite direction, and so on.

Cumulative fatigue is the killer. I once heard a pilot say, when the flying rosters came out for the following month, "Oh dear, oh dear, I might be suffering from roster blindness." "What?" he was asked, to which he replied, holding up his roster, "I can`t 'see' myself doing this!"

But it is not only the pilots who can find flying the line hard; it is also the families, who have to live with or, in reality, without their partner, spouse or parent. Whilst I did not resent the job I did, I was, towards the end of my airline career, extremely conscious of the impact it had on family and friends.

I remember being in Hong Kong, having just checked in from Sydney, feeling sorry for myself. Even though I was now heading in the right direction – home – it was my sons eighteenth birthday that day and I was not there. I really felt bad when I remembered that when he had been born, eighteen years ago to the day, I had also been in Hong Kong.

I recently asked my kids whether they felt I had been an absentee father whilst they grew up. Interestingly enough, my daughter did not see it that way at all. She saw it as a privileged childhood, and one that was full of excitement going to exciting places and having access to the world. She said compared to some of her classmates, who had never been out of the country, she felt like she was the lucky one. That`s kids for you!

What cannot be dismissed is that, compared to the national average, flying does pay well – though this is not the place to get involved in airline employment 'terms and conditions'. Suffice to say, some pay better than others.

The sheer beauty of having an office that allows you to take in the scale and drama of our planet is priceless. Oceans, deserts, mountains, and even the weather itself can be breathtaking; and the journey is never over when you park the aircraft and go to the hotel.

The cities I have been to over the years have left an indelible mark on me, each and every one of them, in their own unique way:

Hong Kong has and always will play a significant part in my life as a city that embraced me with its sheer scale of diversity in culture and texture; a tropical smorgasbord set in the South China Sea. It isn't just the bright lights and vibrant night life, though, as for me it is the street vendors, alleyways, dead rats on the steps in the Chung King Mansions, fishing boats in the harbour at Chung Chow and sitting in Kowloon Park. Walking every inch of a city allows you to get under its skin;

San Francisco to me is the only city in the world where you should drive a '68 Mustang;

New York should only ever be walked, every inch of it, day and night. Soaking it all in;

As one of our cabin crew will testify, never climb Table Mountain, Cape Town, in flipflops;

Don`t for a second think the taxi drivers in Shanghai have ever had driving lessons or know what they are doing;

If you want a decent curry, there is only one place to go in the world: Delhi. But not just for the food, for the people. I have always felt welcome and, most importantly, when you have crew with you, safe;

Los Angeles is the world's largest playground. Within the LA basin you have 2,000 square miles of it. What do you want to do today, on your layover?

I've always believed that whether you have a good trip or a bad trip is down to one person and one person only: you; but then isn't that true of everything in life?

Would I change what I have done with my life? Absolutely not. I feel extremely lucky to not only have had a varied career, but to have flown the line and enjoyed it for what it is. I certainly would not swap it for the 6:22 train every morning to the City for forty years. If that is what you do for a living and you want to change it, I can recommend learning to fly. It could open up the whole world for you, quite literally.

Chapter 14

The Pilots

Flying the line has not changed since the first days of air transport after World War I. The aircraft, yes; the task, the weather, the dangers and the beauty of sunsets, no.

The airlines come and go, with the new kids on the block trying to re-invent the wheel of low cost, no frills, entertainment, video-on-demand, seats that turn into beds. Sixty years ago, the low-cost airlines were the 'red eye' overnight flights from Chicago to Los Angeles; the sleeper services provided real beds, and the entertainment was conversation with your fellow passengers over canapés.

For pilots, the tools of the trade have certainly been refined: weather radar super-imposed on a map display; wind shear warnings and automatic ice detection and removal systems. This does not mean that lives and aircraft cannot be lost to a thunderstorm, a violent microburst or ice, however, for they can and, worse still, they continue to be lost. For no matter how many tools are provided, it is the operator, the pilot, who has to manage these tools in order to navigate a safe path from departure to arrival.

These individuals are line pilots who, by their very nature, have on the whole served their masters and passengers well, and with humility. But it is a lonely profession amongst a sea of people. No longer can the flight deck be shared with bright-eyed children eager to see the myriad of controls, fathers peering over their shoulders equally eager to see. Now Kevlar and armour isolates the line pilot, isolating him to his own world of decision-making.

The very act of going to work is in isolation, too, from the moment of check in. Prior to flight, line pilots assemble in small offices, often deep in the bowels of a terminal building, poring over the reams of documents presented for the flight. In isolation from the airline offices and the rest of the airport, they make decisions that determine the outcome of flight.

Via a side door they exit through a security checkpoint, standing in line with other airport workers, caterers, cleaners and engineers. Should a line pilot be so naïve as to possess a pair of nail clippers, they are confiscated immediately for fear of endangering the flight. Ignored is the trust and confidence placed in the pilot in being behind the controls. Exiting the search area, a line pilot is then transported to their aircraft, which they will be in control of, with or without nail clippers in their pocket.

Continuing pre-flight preparation, interspersed with occasional visits from ground staff requesting signatures for baggage, fuel and load sheets, the line pilot waits, alone.

In isolation, the aircraft is finally manoeuvred over concrete and asphalt to the runway, accelerated to the point of flight, and taken aloft. Cabin crews check on pilots at regular intervals, to ensure they can function for the next ten hours. They provide food and water, opening and closing their cell door when necessary.

But despite this picture painted of loneliness and isolation, there exists a world and sanctuary rich in character and life. For a while, although solitary by design, the line pilot tends not to be solitary by nature. They learn to pace themselves through the sixteen or more hours between bed sheets. The ability to communicate effectively with all those they come into contact with has not been lost, and amongst the sea of pilots that weave around this planet in shoals, exist true characters; different characters with different desires, all sharing the same common bond of flight.

The term 'pilot' is a very broad brush with which to paint a picture, though, as the variety of flying and the variety of skills means that pilots tend to specialize in one particular field.

A pilot can be working in the bush flying medical supplies in and out of primitive strips. Another could be flying freight at night from a European hub, or 500 passengers across the Pacific. Different jobs, different roles, but tied together as a fraternity.

I mentioned humility, and this undoubtedly is the single most important characteristic a pilot can possess, because as any veteran pilot with a CV that looks like an airline directory will attest, you can be chief pilot one day and junior bird man the next if your employer goes out of business. Just because you don't want to haul a Cessna 206 full of fish in your fifties does not mean that you might not have to if you are out of work. It depends on how hungry you are!

The pilots themselves come in all shapes and sizes, sexual orientation, gender, race and religion, too. But the common thread is their passion for their vocation. When and if that is ever lost, then it is time to stop.

Right from the very start, I was surrounded by 'characters', and my brother and I would be in their world whilst we were dragged from one country to the next, catching up with our father, who was drifting around the planet in a Bristol Britannia or a Boeing 707. And in my formative flying career, I certainly came into contact with characters. A lot of the pilots in the 1960s and indeed in the 1970s were veterans of world conflict and had seen not only the glory of flying post-war, but also the pain and anguish.

As mentioned earlier, it was at Long Beach, where I gained my private pilot's licence, that I met another character: the owner of Eagle Aviation, Colleen. She was a formidable lady, who you definitely did not want to get on the wrong side of. In her spare time Colleen raced a Harvard (T6) around pylons in the desert!

In the United States I flew from Bourland Field, a private airport carved out of the prairie by Dick Bourland, an American Airlines captain who looked, walked and talked like Clark Gable, the American actor of the 30s and 40s, most famous for his part in 'Gone With the Wind'.

Bob Satterwhite, also a captain with American Airlines, took me under his wing and, along with his family, supported me in any way they could, not just with good home-cooking but also by allowing me to use his Cessna 182 for instrument training. Based in the Pecan Plantation near Lake Granbury, Bob and Marilyn had their home on a private airport – something in the UK we can only dream of.

Back in the UK, I met up with an Australian pilot whilst undertaking my UK licences and we shared digs in Coventry whilst training. Tony McLellan was originally a crop duster in Queensland, with extensive helicopter experience, particularly on the Bell 47 of the TV comedy M*A*S*H fame. He had a Queen's Commendation for bravery, for pulling people out of floodwaters in Queensland one year. The one thing Tony had in abundance was drive and, coupled with a sharp humour and charm, he was focused. Tony retired from British Airways as a Boeing747-400 captain and now lives back in Australia, running around the Pacific in a Boeing 737.

I flew with so many different people that it would be easy to write a chapter on each and every one of those that stood out. The truth was they all stood out, in their own way.

The test pilots were a classic case in point. We called them 'steely-eyed' because sure as eggs were eggs, if you missed something, they didn't!

The overwhelming memory I have of flying with the likes of George Ellis, Peter Sedgwick, Dan Gurney, Tony Craig and John Horscroft was the effortless way in which they passed on their knowledge, as if by 'osmosis' – or, as the more religious amongst us might refer to it, 'the laying of hands'.

When I look back at some of the flights we conducted as part of the certification programme for the Hawker 1000 they stand out so clearly as remarkable experiences and, in many ways, a privilege to have been a part of.

I have log book entries, just one-liners, that cover these events in abbreviated text; but they fail to convey the enormity of what we were doing:

29th August 1991 in the morning "Test Flight" Vmu
8 landings

29th August 1991 in the afternoon "Test Flight" Vmu
8 landings

3rd September 1991 Upset Manoeuvres "Test Flight"
Vdf #213

4th September 1991 "Test Flight" Vibration Survey #214

6th September 1991 "Flight Test" High Speed Upsets #216

And so it went on.

Vmu means 'minimum unstick' which, if you go on line, can be seen courtesy of Embraer https://www.youtube.com/watch?v=jWIFyH6M5mY   (We were conducting these flights from Woodford near Manchester, and would often use Bedford.)

I never ever went to work during those years thinking, *Hmm, I might be killed today* . . . There was, however, a flight from Woodford that I will never forget.

It was on a Friday afternoon and there was a shortage of pilots. I was asked to fly with a test pilot in a 125 that had been undergoing trials with different settings for the horizontal stabilizer. The test was part of a Vdf/Mdf profile which, in effect, is a dive from altitude. The only problem was that we started to encounter shockwaves forming on the wing over the ailerons. The flight test engineer deduced rapidly what was happening and shouted, "Recover!" at which point the test pilot did exactly that. Confident that no structural damage had occurred, we headed back to Woodford. I remember receiving a formal apology for having been subjected to such an event, as it was later determined the flight should have been conducted with two test pilots and not a mere mortal, such as myself!

This was not the norm, however, as I found that the approach on the whole to the work undertaken was structured and disciplined, with a significant amount of work going into the planning before you even went out to the aircraft.

Production flight test and development flight test are two completely different things. I was fortunate at Hawarden and Woodford to be involved with both, and there was always a pre- and post-flight briefing.

Pre-flight everyone sat around what was in effect a boardroom and went through, step by-step, the flight test profile, which covered everything from start to finish. Sequencing was critical, as fuel burn changes the weight and centre of gravity over time, which meant a profile planned at the end of the flight could not be switched to the beginning. A flight test engineer would sit in between us, undertaking the vast majority of data analysis and recording. In addition, occasionally telemetry data would be transmitted in real time.

The vast majority of flight test is routine; for example, just flying straight and level whilst engine parameters are recorded. However, complacency was never the order of the day, and it was whilst flying with test pilots that – whilst not considering myself in their league and having never been a graduate of a military test pilot school – I found that the discipline they imposed on me helped me time and time again later on in my flying career. The result being that I was fortunate to be allowed to conduct customer acceptance flight tests on brand new A340s in Toulouse with Airbus Industries.

Customer acceptance flight tests are after the manufacturer has completed production flight test and the aircraft is technically 'off test' and could actually just go straight into service. However, some airlines (not all) choose to conduct their own acceptance and follow what Airbus calls a 'CAM' – a flight based on the Customer Acceptance Manual which, for the large part, follows a production flight test schedule.

We would go to Toulouse with engineers, surveyors and lawyers, so that the aircraft could be formally accepted after the flight, with vast sums of money ricocheting from bank to bank around the world. Often these flights would be conducted by fleet management pilots, but as 'technical pilot' for the fleet I would sometimes get asked to carry these out. I loved it.

I was fortunate with my liaison role to be heavily involved with various aircraft manufacturers, and this included Boeing in Seattle. The Boeing 787 was being evaluated, and I travelled out to Seattle on several occasions with engineers to look first-hand at the significant step change in manufacturing technology that was being employed by Boeing.

I always enjoyed Seattle. It is one of those cities that is best described as having 'backbone'. Yes, there are a multitude of industries in the city, and the surrounding area of Puget Sound is steeped in history as a frontier to the Pacific Northwest, but to me it was Boeing that dominated, directly or indirectly, through its suppliers. There was a blue-collar working-class culture within Seattle that took immense pride in its role within the aviation industry, and the pilots and engineers I interacted with at Boeing were always courteous and, again, were unassuming.

Toulouse in France was the same, but with a European twist! It was always a pleasure, as even though years had passed since flying with the test pilots at Bae, I flew with some incredibly competent people at Toulouse as the aircraft still technically belonged to them. I would fly left seat with an Airbus test pilot right seat, and Geoff from our own flight operations department would often act as flight test engineer in the middle.

As well as flying with French and German test pilots, I always enjoyed flying with the two British test pilots, Pete Chandler and Ed Strongman. I knew Pete well, as he had flown with the airline prior to joining Airbus. (He had in the past however been head of the Empire Test Pilot School at Boscombe Down.

Enough said.) Always a pleasure to work with, Pete had a skill which was impressive to an observer: the level of concentration and speed at which he processed information was phenomenal. He also had the enviable ability of being able to turn it on and turn it off whenever he wanted. It is difficult to describe, or put this into context on paper, but it is not too dissimilar to what you see when a sportsman or woman at the peak of their game are shown in slow motion. Pete was always a pleasure to work with.

I was extremely fortunate when I was sent to Toulouse to accompany directors and executives whilst they reviewed the A380. In addition to formal presentations and tours, a flight was laid on by Airbus on a flight test A380 that was also used for passenger demonstrations. Pete Chandler was the captain and, not long after we were airborne, he had me in the right-hand seat.

What an absolute joy. The aeroplane is undoubtedly well balanced with respect to hand flying, and I was immediately struck by how similar it felt to the A320, and not the A330 or A340 family.

The A320 I always felt would sit where you wanted to and, being a narrow-bodied lighter aircraft, was on the whole responsive to changes and corrections, especially close in to a runway.

The A330, and even more so on the A340-600, required a lot more finesse and anticipation when it came to corrections. Some of this I put down to mass, some to geometry, and some to flight control laws for that specific aircraft.

The A380, however, confounded logic, or at least what was logical to me, as it was extremely crisp and responsive without being over sensitive. The deck angles were all extremely comfortable in different configurations and, on the approach, it just felt right.

The conclusion I came to later on, and having pieced some of the puzzle together, was that the aircraft was in fact 'over winged' with respect to both area, loading and high lift devices. The reason being was that it could in theory – though some would argue this was unlikely to ever happen – be stretched, and the additional fuselage plugs would be supported by the same wing without a redesign. A fascinating aircraft, and my extremely brief exposure flying around the South of France along the Pyrenees is one I will always remember.

Pete Chandler went on to conduct the 'first flight' as chief test pilot of the A350 XWB in June 2013. In the flight test world, first flights are significant milestones and one that Pete deservedly accomplished. Airbus has some excellent videos online which are accessible and are well worth watching. In the videos you will see Pete doing what he does best, quietly and professionally.

Ed Strongman led the flight test programme on the military A400M, developing a display routine that to this day is simply jaw dropping. There is an interview on YouTube that for me sums up Ed, as he talks with candour and humility about what he does and includes some display footage which is well worth watching. Ed stands there grinning as if what he does is normal! https://www.youtube.com/watch?v=lU0s_HL8khs

Ed Strongman sadly passed away in 2016. My memory of flying with him is that he would just let you get on with it; yet, without even realizing it was happening, he coached you all the way along. You thought it was your skill, but the reality was it was the person sat next to you, and that was Ed through and through.

There were equally competent men and woman flying the line, who in their own way exemplified everything that, for me, was the best in aviation. There still are.

Some of the trainers were without doubt exceptional and, believe me, as a lot of line pilots will testify, a good pilot does not necessarily make a good trainer! There is something that has to be there within any good training captain, and that is simply a desire to teach. To teach well is still extremely difficult, however, and I do not say this as a trainer but as a student or line pilot on the receiving end.

Not so much today (I hope!) but there was a period of time when a big stick and shouting was the order of the day, certainly in the British army! But as the army, and all organizations will attest, most would say, with hand on heart, that getting the best out of people requires the best being put in to their training.

It was very, very rare, but whenever I found I was on the receiving end of a 'check trapper', I tended to switch my game completely. I would simply switch to 'compliance' mode and just make sure I delivered what was required of me, satisfied the criteria, and went home.

A trainer, however, whilst administering a check ride, would bring out something that was larger than the whole, and I would feel that not only had I given the best I possibly could to the detail, but that I'd got more out of it than I went in with.

There was a training captain who I always held in high regard. As well as a very dry sense of humour – that I was tuned into! – he always made me feel like I wanted to give my best, not simply to please him, but because I owed it to myself.

With a simple one-liner he could put everything into perspective. I recall being on the jump seat whilst a new pilot to the A340 was preparing for departure at Heathrow, and he was going ten to the gallon, rushing as if everything had to be completed ten minutes ago, which it didn't.

The training captain just sat there and didn't say a thing, and the first officer hurriedly grabbed the airfield charts and said, "Are you ready for a brief?"

The training captain said, "Just remember, it`s a bit like taking the *Queen Mary* out of the harbour: everything happens slowly, and we can take as much time as we need to in order to put to sea. Go ahead with your brief."

I remember the first officer looking at him, releasing a huge sigh, and proceeding to provide a thorough, slow brief, slowly and methodically running through the checks, and gracefully taxiing out to the runway without rushing.

I liked that, and I was always conscious of it when we were taxiing at Los Angeles or New York`s JFK and the low-cost carriers were darting around us like the Isle of Wight ferry. *It`s okay, we're in the Queen Mary, and she needs a bit more time and space . . . slow down.*

On extremely rare occasions I would come across someone who was a 'character', but I never ever felt I was with someone who was, let's say, a complete pain in the backside. And I like to think I didn't sit in the latter category! But certainly in the left hand seat you would have to intervene if someone was being a little bit over zealous in the way they spoke to ground staff or cabin crew.

Conversely, there were also pilots you flew with who never seemed to be ruffled.

We had a captain who had been a saxophone player for Manfred Mann's Earth Band and had performed session work with the likes of Diana Ross.

His nickname was 'dormouse'. (He claimed to have plumbed his saxophone into the central heating long ago.) He was a very softly spoken south Londoner from Wimbledon, who would display a hint of excitement whilst pointing out Wimbledon Common on the approach to London Heathrow and, with great pride, say, "It`s all right, Buster, I will be home soon to take you for a walk." He was one of those pilots who gave you the impression he was half-asleep, and yet was as sharp as a razor and didn't miss a trick.

I always enjoyed flying with him as his co-pilot when I first moved onto the fleet, as he would never disappoint, often coming out with no-frills statements that would perfectly sum up any situation at the time.

Coming in from Hong Kong one morning, I was flying the approach. From the time we left Hong Kong to Heathrow, the forecast was for a typical autumn storm, with strong south-westerly winds and horizontal rain. Sure enough, that is what we got, and whilst technically within my crosswind limits as a first officer, it was a horrendous morning.

We pitched and rolled all over London as we swung onto the localizer for one of the westerly runways, with the winds aloft drifting us virtually sideways. There was a momentary gap in the clouds and, picking out Wimbledon Common, he said, "Sorry, Buster, not today," and continued to monitor the instruments as I manfully flew on.

After landing, shaken but thankfully not stirred, we taxied to the gate and shut down. He folded his charts away as if it was but just another day at the office, and turned to me when he had put everything away. Matter-of-factly, he said, "Well, that was exciting, well done. We can go home now, but I think Buster is going to be a bit pissed off, as no way am I going out in that."

Flying and the pleasures which it can provide are not limited to big shiny fancy jets or airliners. Light aircraft and private flying can be just as challenging and just as rewarding and just as memorable.

Stuart McKinnon is an instructor and examiner who commands a lot of respect in our local flying community for being not only competent but oozing confidence by making sure that, above all else, you have fun!

One day, in December 2009 – one of those crisp clear winter days that shape up into a perfect day for flying, irrespective of the temperature – Stuart provided me with an opportunity that I simply could not refuse and, at the end of it, when the sun had set, I had flown three completely different aircraft, and have photographs on my home office wall and memories I will always carry with me.

It started in Shoreham on the south coast by dragging a Piper Tomahawk out. I had not flown one before and was provided a check out as we flew cross-country to Gloucester, where we duly arrived just before lunch. At Gloucester, we pulled out a North American Harvard, which Stuart, as a display pilot and instructor on type, had to get back to Shoreham.

Once airborne, he gave me the aircraft and I was in boy-heaven, running across the south of England consuming more fuel in ten minutes than the Tomahawk had in an hour! Close to a private airstrip on the South Downs in case needed, Stuart also practised his display flying and talked me through as I clumsily attempted to emulate what I had just been shown.

On the ground at Shoreham with the covers on the Harvard, we then pulled out a Bulldog, which is a former British primary trainer for Air Force cadets, and we took off as the sun kissed the horizon to fly along the coast.

What a day. Three completely different aircraft, one unforgettable experience. Thank you, Stuart!

The incredible people I had the pleasure of flying with, laughing and, on September 11th, sharing a tear with, are probably the single biggest thing I miss.

Thank you, all.

Chapter 15

Teamwork

Teamwork is the core to success for any organisation and in any context. It applies to all human endeavours, not just sport, but businesses and even to our personal lives.

Aviation, however, is a safety-critical industry, as is the medical profession, the armed forces, the nuclear industry and manned space flight.

What the public think of first and foremost when you talk about the medical industry, for example, is doctors, nurses, surgeons and consultants. Obviously these are the people we interact with directly in our hour of need, and all focus is on these highly trained professionals; after all, our lives are in their hands.

In many ways, the public look to the pilots and cabin crew they see walking through the airport terminal in the same way. Stepping into the cabin from the jet bridge and into the aisle, a smile from a crewmember and a glimpse through an open cockpit door is confirmation that they are entrusting their lives with these professionals; and this trust has built up between us, as they anticipate their safe passage across the globe, as a direct result of the incredible safety record that has become the norm.

As we know, one of the safest forms of transport, despite the incredible complexity and high-risk that is embedded within it, is flying; and it is by default a high-risk form of travel when you look at what we are actually undertaking, travelling across the sky with a thin layer of various materials separating us from the -56 degrees Celsius atmosphere outside and our cosy cabin, consuming the miles at six miles a minute or more.

So, with respect to teamwork, whilst you see the 'visible' face of aviation when you look at the pilots and cabin crew in the terminal, it is only through immense teamwork that we ever get to be there in the first place.

The next time you arrive early for a flight, instead of plugging into a tablet or phone, find a spot near a window and take a look at what is going on behind the scenes, at what you can see. Just as importantly, take a moment to consider what you can't see, the whole collection of moving parts actually making it all possible, making your flight happen.

There are layers and layers, and thousands and thousands of people making it happen.

When the aircraft comes onto the gate and stops, chocks are put in place, and the pilots are advised that they can release the brakes to allow them to cool following the landing and absorption of energy through friction.

Electricity is connected to allow the Auxiliary Power Unit (APU) to be shut down.

Conditioned air rushes through bright yellow ducting into the aircraft.

Baggage handlers open cargo doors and start unloading onto conveyors the clothes, books, gifts and dreams of many.

A 'honey cart' connects to the underbelly and, with the snap of a lever, human waste is discharged and the toilet tanks are emptied. (Why on earth it is called a 'honey cart' beggars belief.) Separately, water is replenishing the potable water tanks.

Fuel is fed through armoured hoses into the aircraft to give it the energy it needs for further flight – but only after a static discharge line has been connected to the aircraft to prevent a spark and catastrophe.

Engineers walk around carefully inspecting for damage, bird strikes, oil, nitrogen, oxygen and hydraulic levels, tyre and brake wear, to be followed later by a pilot as part of their pre-flight inspection, thus providing the layers of safety we all demand. Double-checking.

If it is winter and the aircraft needs to be de-iced you will see the trucks positioning themselves ready to spray de-icing fluid.

Your bag then rumbles past on a baggage trolley and awaits its turn to be loaded. You see the dispatcher checking the baggage bins and cargo, looking for any identifiable hazardous cargo. Double-checking.

A low vibration resonates across the glass in front of you as a 747 lifts off the runway behind your aircraft, the control tower, manned day and night, clearing the next departure to commence their take off.

Ground control will be clearing the aircraft next to yours to push back and start their engines. The tower controller has already instructed the airborne 747 to contact 'Departure', and in doing so enter the labyrinth of airways, sectors and flight information regions that connect every corner of the planet.

The doors of the fire station are open and, outside, one of six fire tenders is checking equipment. A quick squirt of foam is seen arching out like the tongue of a lizard.

Catering trucks arrive to disgorge blankets and duvets, sandwiches and paninis into your aircraft.

In the distance, an aircraft is being pulled out of a hangar, having spent five days on maintenance with numerous inspections, component changes, software updates, replacement seats and an engine change. You can't see the team who did this, for they are too far away to be picked out against the concrete and steel.

The team that supported the engineers with this task – maintenance planners, parts procurement managers, airworthiness inspectors, quality inspectors, design engineers and mechanics – are in the brick offices beside the hangar.

On the edge of the airport in what looks like a warehouse is a windowless building within which cabin crew training takes place: aircraft mock ups and slides; training and practising for emergencies; sitting inside smoke-filled cabins on jump seats waiting for the announcement "Evacuate, evacuate, evacuate"; or they are forced to conclude that there is no longer a pilot alive to give the command, and initiate the evacuation themselves.

In the next windowless building are simulators within which pilots are practising the normal and non-normal. Simulators that provide incredible realism; that allow them to test their performance, every six months; that allow them to learn and stay on top of their game.

Beyond the trees in a low-slung set of buildings are the airline's offices, the heart of which is the commercial department. These are the strategists and the key to any airline's survival. They look at the yield from different routes, different aircraft and different seasons. They carry out complex modelling on different variables to plan ahead for the next year, two years and ten. Which routes? Which aircraft?

Inside an operations department, covering both ground ops and flight ops within the department, are professional flight planners, crewing and operations staff.

A regulatory affairs department coordinates national and international regulations within the airline, compliance being the key word.

There is a cargo, sales, marketing and press office, making calls, writing for media, creating content.

But that is as far as you can see, just; but that is not the full picture, and you'll have to look further and deeper to see the thousands of men and woman that make up the air transport system.

Aircraft manufacturers look ahead decades in terms of market needs, technological opportunities and threats; and inside any manufacturer you will find thousands of people dedicated to innovation and design, stress engineers, fluid dynamics (aerodynamics) engineers and propulsion engineers. Partnered with engine and avionics manufacturers, the aircraft designers will be looking at applied technology solutions not just for today's air transport needs, but for tomorrow's.

Scratch the surface of any of the above and what you find, strangely enough, is real people. Individual people across the world dedicated to the industry and passionate about what they do. You do occasionally come across the half-empty-glass individual, but on the whole they don't stay within aviation long. It is simply too dynamic and too intense an environment commercially for an employer to carry them.

And we are no different to you, the passenger, in that first impressions count: the receptionist, when you walk into a foyer, sets the tone for your entire experience, before you even start your day, regardless of whether it is in a hotel lobby, airline office or at a check-in counter at the airport terminal.

I was always extremely conscious of that and, as a norm, would always endeavour to join the cabin crew in their briefing and not only introduce myself but encourage them to introduce themselves to me, allowing us to get a feel for each other. The same can be said of most pilots.

On most occasions, we fly with a crew we have never met before and, an hour after meeting them, we are doing a 150mph down a runway together; an hour after meeting we might be asking them to work with us in dealing with an emergency. As a captain, therefore, you want everyone on side – not necessarily to like you and be their 'mate', just to be onside professionally.

I learnt little tricks from other captains over the years in this regard and, on the whole, they seemed to work.

The first thing we did, whenever we walked into the cabin crew briefing room, and apart from knocking on the door and smiling, was to ask the cabin crew manager if it was convenient to enter. This was really important, as they could be right in the middle of a briefing, or questioning someone on a procedure and your timing could be completely wrong! What this also did was show that even though you may be the captain, you respected their environment and did not just barge in.

The next thing we would do was try to spot an empty seat and sit down amongst the crew and be at their level. Standing over people who are sat down is a dominant position to be in, when what you are trying to do is 'engage' with people, most of whom you have never met before. I would always try to acknowledge those that I recognised, too, even if I couldn't remember their name!

Now we could begin.

Crew can be incredibly tribal, and once a crew starts to gel, woe betide anyone who tries to come between them or give them a problem! This is especially true when on the longer trips, to Hong Kong, Shanghai or the west coast of the United States, for instance. You didn't necessarily live in each other's pockets, and do everything down route together all of the time, but if you had a long layover with a free day, someone might organise a trip out.

Any captain who reads this will know exactly what I am talking about when I say that you had to be mindful of your responsibility, even on a layover, as in the eyes of your employer, your crew, and the crew's partners and family back home, you were still responsible for their safety.

Yes, they were all adults, but sometimes crew could be as young as nineteen, and not even legally allowed to drink alcohol in the United States. That was never my biggest concern, however. What worried me the most was when, often simply through ignorance, crewmembers did not have the knowledge or experience when out on the street to realise they were at risk.

As I've shared with you, going to school in Portsmouth taught me a lot about people and how to read the streets; and that, ironically, it was walking around New York City where I never felt uncomfortable, and yet walking around Chicago I was extremely cautious. As for walking around parts of Los Angeles, I just simply would not do it.

There was a safety net when away from the UK, in that we had a station manager and staff at the airport down route that could help deal with any issues. We also had company-approved doctors should medical assistance be required.

There are always going to be the 'characters', however, and it has never ceased to amaze me how many there actually are out there. Everyone has stories about airlines and individuals they have come across in their aviation career, individuals that morph into 'legends' – and some because of their antics on and off an aircraft, and some simply because they were great people to be around.

Some of the best singers on the planet, as witnessed in many a karaoke club, are cabin crew; equally, some of the worst singers on the planet can be found within the crew and, more often than not, it is a pilot who thinks he or she can actually sing!

Entertaining passengers is also a forte of some of the cabin crew, and various 'events' have been shared over the years . . .

The crewmember in business class, who went down the aisle with a desert selection on a trolley, had smeared cake all over her face and was heard to say, "I can recommend the chocolate gateaux."

The crewmember who had deliberately tucked the end of a toilet roll into the top of her skirt and proceeded to unravel the roll as she walked down the aisle, much to the amusement of the passengers.

I was once positioning as a passenger on a B747 into New York's Newark airport, which does not have an exceptionally long runway, and upon landing, with full reverse thrust, firm positive braking and decelerating, a deep masculine voice came over the passenger address from a cabin crew member and said, "Whoooa, big fella, whoooa," at which point the entire aircraft, with nearly 500 people onboard, burst into spontaneous applause.

Air traffic controllers do also, believe it or not, have a sense of humour, and I have heard some interesting exchanges over the years. These days it is rare, though, as everything is posted immediately onto the internet and nothing is sacrosanct anymore, mostly silencing any hint at fun. I have heard this referred to as interference by the 'fun police', and whilst aviation is a serious business, a lot of the humorous events of the past are frowned upon in today's corporate, connected world.

There is something infectious about aviation, and it weaves its way into your very fabric; it becomes part of the very fibre of who you are and what you are. I certainly, for one, do not believe you should overthink it, but just enjoy it for what it is, and never *ever* forget that nobody is God's gift to aviation. At the end of the day, it is teamwork that not only makes it happen, but allows you to do the thing you love doing, whatever that may be.

So the next time you are in the boarding area, take a look outside, and if there is a five-minute delay, ask yourself if it really matters. It may just be the five minutes someone out there needs to keep you safe.

Chapter 16

Politics of the Air

Politics.

I hate politics.

But then everyone says that, even the politicians, and whether we like it or not, we simply cannot escape it, as regardless of our profession it affects everything we do, locally, nationally and internationally. Aviation is no different, and even at the beginning, legislation and rules were introduced and they in turn had to be enforced, ultimately by governments, which is full of politicians.

After World War I, it was quickly recognised that controlling air power in times of peace was as equally as important as in times of war.

In the United States, first with Postal Services and later with flying boats, it was realised that spheres of influence on a national level could be expanded exponentially. In the United Kingdom, the British Empire, whilst being supported with a powerful merchant fleet, soon recognised the benefits of aviation for supporting long lines of communication.

Bilateral agreements and route licences allowed countries to manage and, most importantly, control who had access to the trunk routes.

Pan Am (Pan American) dominated internationally for the United States, and Imperial Airways, later to become BOAC (British Overseas Aircraft Corporation), eventually evolving into today's British Airways, supported UK interests. Air France, Lufthansa, Qantas and JAL (Japanese Airlines) all represented their respective national interests.

Even today, with airlines such as Emirates and Qatar, for example, national interests are met and in turn connect people and trade.

The negative from all this is that political influences can have a devastating effect on start-ups and new ventures into established markets. Probably the best example in my mind is that of British Caledonian Airways (BCal), one of my former employers.

The late Sir Adam Thomson, the founder of BCal, wrote an autobiography called High Risk: The Politics of the Air, which encapsulates all of the above and puts it into perspective.

The brutal reality is that policies, and decisions made by politicians, impact and influence everyone within the industry, and something as simple as granting or denying a route licence can make or break some operators.

At the coal face, however, the employees of an airline have absolutely no influence or control over the long-term survival of their employer. For airline employees in particular this can have devastating ramifications when it comes to providing for a family.

If your employer suddenly ceases trading and you are out on the street, so too are hundreds if not thousands of your colleagues, all chasing what few jobs there are. Align that to national boundaries and licencing, and it means that an American pilot cannot seek work in the UK, or a British pilot seek work within Australia without possessing the 'right to abode' and a work permit.

Within the UK, over time, there have been waves of redundancies as operators either fold or are swallowed by competitors. I remember pilots once being referred to by a senior manager as being like 'pebbles on a beach'. When I asked what on earth he meant by that, it was explained to me that whenever there is a storm at sea, the waves that roll in wash up new pebbles, to be picked up by employers . . . sadly it is true, for when an airline folds, the competitors pick up the pebbles they want and leave the rest to wait, more often than not determined simply by the type rating held on your licence.

I recall when we were given thirty days' notice at Nov Air International, having just completed a DC-10 course with two hours forty-five minutes in my log book, complaining bitterly to a captain that this was my fourth employer that would be disappearing into the annals of aviation history. He just laughed and said it was his twelfth!

Since then, within the United Kingdom, Dan Air, Air UK, British Midland, Excel and Monarch have all gone. In the United States, Eastern, Braniff International, Pan Am, Piedmont, Continental, Allegheny have disappeared, and many others.

The politics are not just limited to the air, however, as they have just as significant an impact on the ground.

Airports are themselves under constant attack from other vested parties due to either the tremendous aggregate value from crushing concrete and extracting gravel, or for housing and property development opportunities. Indeed, Hatfield, where I was based with British Aerospace, no longer exists as an airport, the irony being that Sir Geoffrey de Havilland had faced the same threats at Stagg Lane, his London base of aircraft operations, and moved everything to Hatfield as it was so far out of London it couldn't possibly be affected!

The lack of political backbone on the ground has resulted in Heathrow, for example, being overstretched where it is arguably no longer fit for purpose due to a lack of runways; and general aviation airfields are constantly being either closed or stalked for housing.

Within any business there is of course internal politics, and that can be as damaging, not because of its existence, but if it is not recognised. It has taken me a long time to recognise this, and that is simply because when it comes to company politics, by my own admission, I am not very good at it! This may stem from my training as an engineer and, as we all know, trying to apply structure, order and logic to some situations simply does not work.

It requires influence and a political willingness to engage when it comes to finding solutions and, most importantly, the ability for a leopard to change its spots – not in a negative way, but having the ability to recognise when changes are required both internally and externally. Some people are masters at what we often refer to on this little island of ours as being able to 'read the tea leaves'!

For any business to survive, especially in the airline industry, you need not only leaders but also managers to deliver change all the way through the decades, regularly. The airlines that do, survive. Those that lose their political sphere of influence and fail to adapt, die.

I had first-hand experience of such a scenario. In 1990, having been made redundant from Nov-Air International, I was determined not to get caught in the roller coaster of the airline industry, and thought I had found pilot 'Nirvana' when I joined British Aerospace Commercial Aircraft and worked on the corporate jet programmes. Bae: exciting, challenging work embedded within the heart of the UK industry. As stated in an earlier chapter, surely working for Bae would be safe as houses, right? Wrong. I'll now explain why in more detail.

British Aerospace had diversified to the point where it was a political and financial basket case and behind the scenes, unbeknown to any of us, plans were being put in place to separate from the things that took money – Rover cars, for example – and inject cash through sales of divisions that were attractive to others.

Bae had split its businesses on the civil aviation front into Bae Regional Aircraft, which the Bae 146, ATP and Jetstream programmes came under. Bae Airbus managed the design and manufacture of the wings for Airbus production in Toulouse. Bae Corporate Jets Ltd covered the 125 business jet. On 1st May 1992, Bae was removed from the name and it was simply called Corporate Jets Ltd. At the same time it announced that it was seeking a buyer or, alternatively, a majority partner.

In September that year, the annual industry event, the NBAA (National Business Aircraft Association) convention, was held at Dallas, Texas, in the United States. At this juncture it was announced it was withdrawing from offering the company for sale as "We are pleased that the uncertainty surrounding Corporate Jets' future has been removed."

Not quite true. Politics.

The real reason for the withdrawal was due to challenges around trying to sell the company, which had to be resolved first. (These were for both legal and political reasons.)

The first move was to make Corporate Jets a subsidiary of British Aerospace Inc, and move the headquarters from Hatfield to the Bae-owned Arkansas completion centre in Little Rock, Arkanasas – a place I was very familiar with as a result of ferrying aircraft across the Atlantic from Chester (Hawarden). Not surprisingly, US citizens featured heavily in the management team. In December 1992, Bill Boisture, an American citizen, was appointed president and CEO.

In January 1993, I was positioned to Washington DC and flew with Bae Inc pilots to South America as part of a sales demonstration tour of the new Corporate 1000, a long-range business jet. We flew all over Brazil, visiting Recife, Sao Paulo (Conconhias), Fortaleza , Maringa, Belo Horizante and Rios Santos Dumont. But I started to see the writing on the wall, and had fortunately by then been in aviation long enough to know what was coming.

On 1st June 1993, Bae announced that it had agreed to sell Corporate Jets to Raytheon of the United States and call it Raytheon Corporate Jets Inc. Whilst not announced at the time, and it did not actually take place until 1994, was the transfer of production from Chester to Wichita. Raytheon owned Beechcraft and, sure enough, in September 1994, Raytheon Aircraft Company, a $1.7 billion business, was created combining Beechcraft and Hawker.

A year earlier, seeing what was coming, I flew with John Horscroft, the chief test pilot at Hatfield, from Deauville back to Hatfield having been to Geneva, Switzerland, earlier that day demonstrating an 800 series 125 to a potential customer. It was officially my last flight, as on 11th October I joined Virgin Atlantic Airways to start training on the Airbus A340.

At the time, Virgin had four aircraft (747s), and was about to embark on an expansion plan that not only included Airbus A340s but also new Boeing 747-400s. How long could this employer last?

I was now thirty-three, with yet another company notched on my belt. Politics had again impacted me directly, and Corporate Jets (the Crown jewels as far as we were concerned) had been sold off to the United States and had injected much-needed cash into Bae. It was not long after I left Bae that Hatfield shut down and was subsequently sold off and redeveloped.

Friday 8th April 1994 was Hatfield's last day as an airfield, when a DH Chipmunk, the type that had made the first landing on the new runway, was also the last plane to take off from the main runway, followed by a DH Tiger Moth – carrying a de Havilland Flag – which took off from the grass at the side of the runway.

When I joined my new employer as a first officer, and was sent off to Miami for an initial Airbus course, I did not have a lot of confidence that I would retire from what was just another relatively new airline. Sir Richard Branson was to prove me and the industry spectacularly wrong, however, by proving that both he and the people around him were extremely adapt at 'reading tea leaves' and, most importantly, understood the 'politics' of business.

But when Lord King and British Airways homed in for the kill, having swallowed BCal and Dan Air as if they were mere appetisers, they spat Virgin out when the tables were turned, with the revelations of the infamous 'dirty tricks campaign'. Having seen and having been on the receiving end before of political fallout, if my new employer could fight the fight when it came to business politically, what about the ever-changing market?

The difference this time around was in the fact that my new employer had the skills required to change with the times – what I call the 'Madonna effect'! Madonna, as a pop icon, has over the years transformed seamlessly from one character and style to the next. David Bowie did the same, and in doing so was able to bridge generational changes and audiences.

Virgin did this with products and service. Brilliantly.

As pilots we had absolutely no influence on this, however: it was all going on behind us in the cabin.

Being a small airline it could design, develop and introduce products far more quickly than competitor long-haul operators. One of the cabin design engineers once explained to me that if they wanted to change a fascia on a bar module, for example, the entire fleet could be retrofitted as they went through hangar maintenance checks over a six-month period. A large airline with different fleets, maintenance providers and bases could take years.

This ability to respond rapidly and introduce technological changes in the cabin kept the company at the cutting edge in terms of product and design. Harness this with good marketing and brand delivery, and you have a winner.

Strategic positioning and posturing continues to this day with nations and airlines, and as a direct result of mergers and acquisitions. As employees you have very little, if indeed any, input or say in what is going on around you; you just hope that you backed the right horse and try to do your job to the best of your ability.

I was fortunate in so much as the roles I became involved with in the companies I worked for were fairly disciplined and engineering biased. Unfortunately, though, you would have to on occasion stand your ground as departmental battles raged around you. But that is business, and true for any business. In fact that is society, and any society!

It was the late nineteenth century historian, Lord Acton, who said: "Power tends to corrupt; absolute power corrupts absolutely." Reputedly, even the Roman Empire recognised this problem and had it carved in Latin on Senate chambers.

I remember once being accused of being 'ambitious', which at the time I was taken aback by, as it was the last thing in the world I thought of myself as. I realised, however, that from the outside looking in, it probably did look exactly like that. But for me it was simpler, in as much as I enjoyed what I did, and had an insatiable appetite for it, so what I did was completely and unashamedly grasp opportunities. I was also extremely lucky in that I worked for people I had a great deal of respect for, and the opportunity to learn from them was something I was not going to miss.

Without a doubt, politics in any form is part of life, and as individuals you have to choose to what extent you do or don't get involved. In many respects you can isolate yourself when flying, because the task in hand, at that particular moment in time and on that particular day, is safely flying an aircraft from A to B.

On the ground I saw an opportunity and started an FBO (fixed based operator), handling business and general aviation aircraft at a former military airfield, and the business grew rapidly, becoming very successful. However, by this stage in my life, I had accumulated a lot of experience when it came to reading the tea leaves, and I had concerns about the long-term sustainability of the business. I therefore concluded that it would be in everyone's best interests to shut it down and support all of the staff with placement within the industry, which we subsequently achieved.

I was repeatedly challenged by people as to why I did not stay and fight, which was extremely easy to answer: you have to fight the battles that you are confident you will win.

The airline industry is rife with rumour and gossip 24/7. We used to refer to it as 'Galley FM'. (The current version is 'fake news', where not everything being fed to us is necessarily correct and factual.) You could guarantee that at 2 o'clock in the morning, somewhere over the Atlantic or the jungles of Africa, you would be told the latest 'hot news' when you went out to stretch your legs and get a drink in the galley: "Straight up, one of the engineers told me at JFK last week! Also Chip told me at breakfast at the car park hotel. It has to be true!"

In New York we all tended to stay at a hotel on Long Island, which is located in a massive car park next to a stadium. To the crew it was simply known as 'the car park hotel'. With so many flights a day to JFK from London, and operated by both Airbus and Boeing fleets, it was a melting pot of people and a fertile feeding ground for rumours and 'hot news'.

At the centre of all of this was the aforementioned 'Chip', who was a waiter in the hotel restaurant and served all of the crews. Chip was a very affable and, shall we just say, a talkative man . . . the 'breaking news' source of choice before social media took a hold. If you wanted to know what routes we were about to start, what aircraft we were going to order, and how many, we asked Chip.

Politics. Don`t you just love it . . .

Chapter 17

20 West

The canopy of stars hangs above us in an arc resembling the ceiling of an omni-theatre. In the distance, the first turquoise of dawn starts to appear, defining the curvature of the planet, except there is no land mass to illuminate, just the vast North Atlantic Ocean.

The heavy Airbus A330 ripples like a serpent across the cobblestones of the meandering ribbon of the jet stream that swirls around the planet, heading east.

"Anyone approaching 20 west with a ride report," calls out an American voice somewhere ahead of us.

On the navigation display I can see two aircraft on our track ahead, 1000 and 2000 feet above. Sixty miles to the north is a TCAS position display of an aircraft at the same level, flight level 360. We are all on the night organised track system that forms an Atlantic bridge between North America and Europe. (During the day the track system is orientated for westbound traffic.)

I like TCAS. Not only does it do the job of providing vertical guidance to avoid other aircraft and act as a last chance safety net, it also works as a 'fish finder', telling you who else is around you travelling at six miles a minute, or more. Very handy.

Broken transmissions can be heard – ". . . zul . . . twe . . . vere . . . thr . . .f . . ." – and then clearly: "Yep, American 50 is on Yankee approaching 25 west and continuous moderate chop flight level 340."

The broken transmission is too far away for us to pick up what they're saying, but it sounds like it's on track Zulu.

The vertical speed indicator oscillates up and down, ever so gently. Looking up again I can see the reflection of the centre instrument panel on the glass of the windscreen. Turning to the left, all I can see is my own reflection staring back at me.

The distance to go to the next waypoint is counting down nice and quickly, the groundspeed approaching 600 knots – over 650mph. We are taking full advantage of the jet stream as it curves east at our latitude. Distance to go is going from double to single digits as we approach 30 west. At 30 west we will cross from Gander to Shanwick at the mid-Atlantic point.

At 20 west I will be grabbing a bowl of chopped fruit for breakfast, or maybe even a cooked breakfast if there is one spare from the business cabin. Coming off the ocean, we will switch to Shannon for radar identification and hopefully a direct routing to Liffy. It is always 20 west where I feel I am nearly home, still with ocean in front, though, but with the vast majority of the Atlantic behind us.

Right now, however, the Satcom link with Gander has terminated and a log on confirmation comes up for EGGX, Shanwick. Satellite communication, Satcom, allows us to stay connected without the vagaries of HF communication bouncing off the ionosphere – a positive step forward in technology, everyone agrees.

As the radar sweeps across the navigation display, a wisp of green brushes across, as though it were a sweep of an artist's brush depicting the fingers of some hideous ghoulish sea monster. The radar sweeps back and the fingers become more defined. I tilt the radar down half a degree in manual mode and reduce the range. There appears the tell-tale red of weather cells, two of them slightly to the right, two eyes peering out from the green on the screen in front of me. In silence, the first officer puts his finger on the seatbelt sign and I just nod, my eyes having picked up the TAT readout measuring total air temperature of the air mass through which we were flying. It was rolling back and forward; now it is rolling in one direction only, showing that we are flying into warmer air.

The aircraft pitches up slightly, and the thrust increases as the autopilot and auto thrust compensate for the warmer, less dense air as 30 west slides beneath us. The Canary Islands are to the south, a long way south.

With a howl, the aircraft pitches up again, and the engines spool up. With a sharp jolt, the aircraft shudders.

Looking at the big navigation display in front of me, I can see where the other aircraft are on our track, and even though we were on centre line, there are aircraft in front of us, offset by one and two nautical miles respectively to the right. I can see that even though they are above us, it is extremely unlikely that we are nibbling at the descending wake turbulence corkscrewing behind them. Invisible in the twilight, the jet stream is too strong to allow it anywhere near us. I am sure the pitching is just Mother Nature prodding us.

Gently the Airbus pitches over a little more, and locks onto its pre-set altitude, as if on rails. My knees press the outsides of the foot well, gently, my left knee against the sidewall panel and the right against the centre consul. This is a brace position that, unconsciously, on reflex, I have momentarily adopted. I am unsure whether this is in fear or due to a subconscious desire to feel the airframe course through my body, acting as a pair of sensor pads to connect me with the outside world. Soon, however, it is no longer needed and I feel my legs relax as we settle comfortably into calm air.

The green shards across the display slide to the bottom of the screen, and the red cells are no longer visible with the current tilt angle of the radar, indicating we are above the core cell areas and not at risk. The smooth ride allows us to sail east, into the dawn.

As the sun, masquerading as a 200-billion-watt light bulb, rises above the horizon, I can feel the barbs of light piercing the back of my eyes. My core body temperature has dropped, and I know I am at the lowest point in terms of fatigue I could possibly be. (Any long-haul pilot will tell you in detail the feeling of grit in their eyes when the world changes from total darkness to intense brightness as the sun sits on your horizontal plane, burning into you relentlessly.)

The seatbelt signs are off and one of the crewmembers comes in to check on us and, on cue, says, "Blimey, it`s bright in here!" The first officer and I just catch each other's grin as we both share the same thought: *Really*? If we had a pound, or even a dollar, for every time someone has come in from a dark cabin, a world of blankets and duvets, muted chimes and faint hues of colour bouncing off the ceilings from screens rerunning films for new audiences, and said exactly that, we would be very wealthy.

With our breakfast orders taken, and the sun now midway up the cockpit window, I reflect not on the view but the journey, where I am right now, at four thirty in the morning over the Atlantic staring down at the ocean, upon which ships have traversed for centuries, submarines have stalked, and lives have been saved or lost.

It is just over a year since that bizarre approach, where I was convinced that the New York Port Authority had completely lost the plot and painted a snow-covered airport with black stripes in the vain hope that it would improve aviation safety and make it easier for anyone approaching out of the freezing night.

I had found myself, several weeks later, embraced in the safety net that our airline provides when it needs to manage medically grounded pilots: sitting on a bench in front of a church just south of Harley Street in London, having just come out of the eye clinic, and still in shock having been told I had a retinal tear. It was a beautiful early spring day, and London had taken on a beauty that lifts the soul and nourishes the spirit post-winter. Walking through Green Park earlier, tourists and students had been stretched out on the grass as I cut diagonally across on the path, leaving Buckingham Palace behind me. Everything was a blur, sitting outside that church, quite literally. I'd had eye drops put in both eyes for the examination, and they had dilated my pupils to the extent that the light was excruciating, even with sunglasses on.

I struggled to find my flight crew manager's number on my phone and managed, eventually, to auto dial and share the news that had left me feeling very alone and very confused: I'd received a letter from the Civil Aviation Authority that rescinded my flying privileges until such time as my medical certificate was reinstated. This letter had had a huge impact on me, reminding me that, at fifty-five years old, I was actually mortal . . . and life wasn't meant to be fair.

Due to my technical background, I was asked to undertake a ground-based project in the meantime, writing EASA Part B, operations manuals for all four aircraft and variants we operated, the B747-400, A340-600, B787-9 and A330-300. I would also undergo further tests and evaluations in order to return to flying duties with a first-class medical certificate.

The prognoses from a medical perspective was good, as it was determined fairly early on that the retinal tear was in fact an old event that may have actually occurred decades earlier. I was asked if I had ever participated in bungee jumping, or taken a blow to the head. The answer to both of which was a resounding no! Whatever had caused it was immaterial, however; the fact was I had this tiny hole in my left eye described as a 'very shallow retinal detachment with an ovoid retinal break'. 'Vitreous haemorrhage inferiorly', it turned out, was the black lines that I had seen in my field of view that night approaching Newark's Liberty Airport.

After numerous tests and monitoring it was concluded that I could return to flying, as my binocular vision – in other words, vision with both eyes – was perfectly normal, the caveat being, however, that my medical would have a multi-crew limitation initially, meaning I had to fly with a co-pilot for commercial air transport. Not a problem, as we operated two crew as a minimum. Further examinations later followed and, as a result, a full unrestricted medical was reinstated.

And here I am . . . flight level 360, back in the seat, in command of an airliner, feeling like death warmed up, waiting for the sugar rush from a bowl of fruit so I can pull the required energy levels together for an approach. The miles continue to count down, silently, towards 20 west.

Yet there is something wrong, very wrong, and this is the first time in my entire career I feel at risk. Something is gnawing at me that I just can't not shake but, more importantly, I cannot change. I feel a fear that has now risen to a crescendo.

In my flight bag is a copy of a report I had printed off from the Clinical Practice Guideline for Retinal Detachment and Similar Conditions, developed for the Aerospace Medical Association by their constituent organisation, the American Society of Aerospace Medicine Specialists. In the paragraph headed 'Medical Concerns' there is a statement that reads:

'These sequelae are obviously key concerns for adequate performance in aviation or special

operations duty. Furthermore, consideration must be given to the risk of recurrence or involvement of the fellow eye based on the etiology (as described above).'

http://www.asma.org/home
http://www.asams.org/guidelines/Completed/
NEW%20Retinal%20Detachment.htm

Recurrence. . .

I had raised this concern throughout the previous year, and it always seemed to be discounted on the basis that I would continue to be monitored, and 'no change' was the basis on which I was re-issued a medical certificate. But now I was back in an environment that regularly pressurized my body and its organs, and at the end of each flight I had a half-drunk plastic water bottle that looked like it had been strangled due to the effects of pressurization. Yet the common answer I received when I mentioned this was: 'There is no evidence to suggest that pressurization has a detrimental effect on retinal detachments.'

But I knew a pilot who, having returned to flying duties, had suffered further complications resulting in very unpleasant surgery. In addition, when I returned to flying I kept hearing, "Oh yeah, so-and-so had that as well . . ." by the end of which I concluded this was not uncommon in the flying community.

Having spent my career to date determining my own conclusions based on the data in front of me (back to the engineering DNA), it was pretty obvious that I was being told the truth and the 'data spread' was not sufficient yet to reach any conclusions. But I also suspected it would be another twenty years before a research graduate at a university would look at the industry and conclude the obvious: flying long-haul as a career is not a healthy occupation! I likened it to lead in paint: it was not until there were enough premature deaths that the data actually meant anything. A sobering thought.

The sun by now has reached a plane above the cockpit and shines directly on to the top of my legs. The instrument panel has a triangular shaft of sunlight illuminating the screens. In front of me sits the clock, just above my right knee, and I am inexorably drawn to it, staring at each second advancing. Remembering what had been seared into my consciousness, and conscience, decades before by American Airlines pilot Bob Satterwhite in Texas, the clock remains the most important instrument on the flight deck. The seconds advance some more and, as the chime of the cockpit door alert echoes around me, the truth dawns on me: it is time to take control of the most important instrument in life . . . the clock.

It is time to stop long-haul flying.

The cockpit door opens and one of the crew, carrying our breakfast, steps in and says, "Blimey, it`s bright in here . . ."

Chapter 18
The Greenwich Meridian

I find myself, two years' later, within a world that has been reduced to minutes of longitude rather than degrees. Below Greenwich, travelling south on the 0 degree meridian by approximately fifty miles, I wander no further west than one degree.

Route 66 is known as 'The Mother Road', traversing east to west across the great plains of the United States; in West Sussex, we have 'The Other Road', the A272 that traverses east to west across the heart of the South Downs National Park.

Anybody who retires or leaves a profession as intense as aviation will tell you that it takes time to adjust; and service men and women know only too well how hard it can be to assimilate within family and the real world after decades of service. Whilst I have never been in a combat environment, never been shot at or sat on the bottom of an ocean in a submarine, the challenges I have faced over the last two years have been in some cases not what I expected!

The first six months and, to a lesser extent even now, sleep has been a challenge. Being in the same time zone and not being strapped in an aircraft at 4 o'clock in the morning has certainly caused sleepless nights, and the most vivid flying dreams I have ever had. At night I find myself in the corners of my subconscious, physically flying, managing aircraft and systems, or in airports and hotels solving problems! I am sure a psychiatrist would have a field day with this.

But all I can put it down to is the fact that for my entire career I was immersed in a profession that took a lot of thought processes, and within my head is a mechanism that has suddenly been told it is no longer required. During the day, whilst remaining active and stretching myself, at night it is as if the brain says, *Okaaay . . . that is all well and good, but there is all this data and information that needs to be used*, so off it goes, galloping away, putting me back in an aircraft, back over the Atlantic and back in control.

Even though I had a period of several months on the ground following the initial loss of my medical, I was still immersed in aviation. I was driving daily to London Gatwick to the airlines offices, writing manuals, talking to pilots, and I continued to be surrounded by an airline. It was when I physically left, and put my flight bag away, that the finality of it all hit me. I was not even sure what my professional status was when filling in the part of 'Profession' on car insurance applications . . .

Having another string to my bow, however, has without doubt probably been the best thing I have ever done; and it was having something to hold onto that first year that gave me the stability I needed to transition away from airline employment.

Some people have hobbies – golf, sailing, tennis or other interests – that allow them to channel time and energy into the continuation of a lifelong pursuit, or even start something new. I have always been interested in business, however, and from the early days as a propulsion development engineer have been heavily involved in commercial activities. As well as aviation ventures, I also, in parallel, built up a commercial real estate business that has occupied time whilst alone in hotel rooms around the world, and put me in a position where, when faced with the opportunity to retire, I could afford to do so.

It was the year 2000, when I was transiting from the classic B747-200 to the B747-400, that an opportunity presented itself to purchase a poultry farm in West Sussex.

A large agricultural company owned the farm, along with approximately one hundred other farms across the UK, and had decided to dispose of most of their assets. The reason being that with expansion of the European Union and the future access to the UK markets of countries with a lower cost base, it followed that poultry production would be hammered in the domestic market. Why? Because the supermarkets would choose to purchase from the cheapest source within Europe. Why shouldn't they? Supermarkets had already shown that they were aligned to shareholders first and foremost and not to the farmers. It therefore followed that UK poultry farms or, for that matter, within any agricultural sector, the UK would struggle to compete against European products costing a fraction of the cost to produce.

The farm we purchased was a 'broiler farm', producing poultry for consumption (not eggs), and could hold a maximum of 120,000 birds at any one time per cycle. (The farm averaged 750,000 birds per annum.) It required significant capital investment to build new poultry houses and grow the site capacity to 200,000 birds per cycle in order to be commercially viable, something it was surmised by the previous owners that needed to be done across the whole country and they were clearly not prepared to do.

What we saw, however, was not a chicken business but a real estate opportunity in the southeast of England at a time when London, and the country as a whole, was on the verge of growing. We purchased the site and, for four years, produced poultry for the supermarkets, whilst obtaining planning consent for conversion to industrial units. Some of the buildings we simply bulldozed and built modern factory units in their place.

In 2004, we stopped the agricultural use. As predicted, the agricultural industry in the United Kingdom underwent dramatic changes, and most farms either ceased production or diversified. A lot of the small dairy units went, and with it people's livelihoods and a way of life.

When we took the property on, most people thought we were nuts and had completely lost the plot. I was adamant, though, that with the volatility of the airline industry nobody owed me a living, and it was up to me to make sure I always had a 'get out of jail card' and the ability to earn an income. (Final salary pension schemes do not exist anymore, and I was not working in the public sector with any form of security.) I was not alone with this mindset, and you will find a lot of pilots have business interests outside of flying. I remember that one of our captains, in his forties, had built up a plumbing business and was living in the Cotswolds. One day he just quit. When I asked him why, he responded very simply: "To be home every night with my family."

So, for the first year after retiring from long-haul flying, I threw myself into the business and became more involved. It gave me a purpose and provided a structure for my day.

The other thing I threw myself into is the thing that has been the biggest and most positive change to my new way of life: family and friends.

My daughter summed it up very well, I thought, as only a nineteen-year-old university student studying Psychology can. When I asked her what it has been like having me around more, and not just being around for a couple of days in between trips, jet lagged and fatigued, she replied: "Oh it`s great, Dad . . . you`re not so much of an arse!"

Well, that told me.

Being around and spending time with people close to me has been something that, without doubt, I cherish, and has set me up for the years ahead. It has allowed me to spend time with my father, talking to him about his experiences, his perspective and his career in aviation, something that just simply had to be heard and something that had to be recorded.

But engineering has always been a core part of me as a person; and an interest in all things mechanical has always been a part of my life and continues to be so. In the last year, I have restored a motorbike, and tinkering away in my garage-come-workshop, has given me immense pleasure. And currently I have a 1967 wire-wheeled MG Midget in pieces, with the body stripped and repaired. A long-term project!

Recently designated as a National Park, the South Downs is where I am drawn to in moments of solace, and allows me to reflect not on the past but on the future, for I have always been a glass half-full person, and never dwell on the emptiness left behind. But in the winter months, when the weather is too foul to venture out onto the South Downs or into the Sussex countryside, my garage can provide the solitude which I do still occasionally need. I prefer it over the loneliness of a hotel room!

I am very fortunate, and I do not for a second think otherwise. I am fortunate to have, certainly for now, good health, and to have been part of an industry that has changed the landscape upon which we stand by connecting the planet and allowing barriers such as race, creed and spheres of influence to be turned on their head.

'Globalisation' is a word often used by politicians and world leaders to elicit fear within the human psyche and, in effect, isolate us from the rest of humanity. There are examples all over the world: in China, the Great Wall; in the United Kingdom, Hadrian's Wall; and if the current president of the United States gets his way, a 'Border Wall' separating two nations.

However, aircraft know no boundaries or limitations. Lines on a map might delineate the influence of man on paper, but not on the planet, for it is merely a sphere which we all share.

It is up on the Downs where perspective can be given to our planet – and is England at its most quirky, for only in England are you able to be 'up' on hills that you call 'the Downs'!

To the south lies the English Channel, clearly visible on a clear day, sweeping west past the Isle of Wight and out into the open North Atlantic. Arcing above, emerging out of both London's Gatwick and Heathrow airports, aircraft climb southbound, switching frequencies to either Paris or Brest control when they reach mid-channel.

Impossible to see in the distance, to the north, is Guildford, nestled in the Surrey Hills. There resides a connection with the future – space – for on a business park, within a modern factory, research, development and manufacturing takes place for satellites; technologies that, when harnessed with developments around the world, will connect planets on a scale and in a way that were once the dreams of Science fiction.

Do I feel positive about the future of the aerospace industry? Yes.

Do I feel disappointed at the standing engineering and aerospace has within society? Yes. Disappointed that in today's social media revolution, reality television and blogging culture, real skills and talents are consigned to the bottom of the page.

Recently, whilst scrolling through the news on my tablet, I noticed a headline at the top relating to a fox hunting vote being dropped by the UK prime minister. Below was an article about a social media spat between

KFC and McDonalds over the size of their respective burgers. I then spotted an article tucked into the Science and Environment tab that said: 'John Young dies at 87.'

The saddest thing about the death of John Young is that the editors who placed the article right at the bottom of the page, which you would only find by scrolling all the way through burgers and French fries, were probably right to have placed it where they did . . . for the vast majority of their news feed audience would not have a clue who John Young was.

For the record, John Young was the only astronaut to have flown missions on the Gemini, Apollo and Space Shuttle programmes. He flew to the moon twice. On Apollo 10, the mission was to fly to the moon as a rehearsal for the Apollo 11 landing two months later. The crew tested the lander module in lunar orbit without landing it. They were the first to see the dark side of the moon.

John Young walked on the moon himself in 1972, as commander of the Apollo 16 mission. He became the ninth person to have set foot on the moon. There have only ever been twelve pairs of footsteps on the moon.

He was reprimanded by NASA for smuggling a corned beef sandwich on one mission, which he handed to fellow astronaut Gus Grissom whilst orbiting Earth.

In 1981, he commanded the inaugural flight of Columbia, the first space shuttle. In 1983, he commanded Columbia on the first Spacelab mission.

It is because of people like John Young that I do feel positive about the future, regardless of where their obituary resides in the press.

When I stop and look at what is happening around the planet with the development of space technologies in not just Europe, Russia and the United States, but also in India and China to name but two, I find it heartening to see that the atmosphere, like a line on a map, is invisible to applied technology and human endeavour, regardless of national identity.

If you want to get a sense of the sheer scale, diversity and raw power of what is taking place right now, search on the internet and take a look at Space X, Dream Chaser, Blue Origin and Virgin Galactic. The world is connected through commerce and technology, through spirit and passion, through time and space.

So, if having read this book to the final sentence, and you share my reason to wonder about the world and its future, and have a fire in your belly, too, and view life as an adventure, I say simply: Never forget that for all of us life is terminal, so for your sake and your sake alone, get out there and live your dream . . .

Chapter 19

A Licence to Learn

The yellow nose with its 260hp engine throbbing in front of the firewall pitches up as I pull on the stick. I can feel the back pressure increasing as the Perspex canopy fills with blue sky, and the very slight buffet from the wings. The dark hue of the sky signifies winter, with a low sun and darkness beyond its reach. The coast along Selsey to the south of Goodwood aerodrome acts as a site line for us as we transit east to west, climbing to altitude and then spinning back down.

The Slingsby T67M was designed as a primary trainer, and used successfully by the UK armed forces and various countries; though following several fatal accidents in the United States, the US Air Force disposed of their aircraft in 2006, cutting them up. Its wings and monocoque structure are primarily all composite, with very thin high-performance wings that lend itself to aerobatics.

Jos is beside me, with his hand covering his stick, having just demonstrated a spin recovery after spinning to the left. The rapid departure from the stall with full left rudder input had come as a surprise, not because of the tumbling rotating perspective it had presented, but the speed with which the spin had developed as it transitioned from the first spiral.

I had spun aircraft before. This, however, was different.

I can feel the buffet as we approach the stall, progressively pulling the stick all the way into my lap and, at the point of the aerodynamic stall, I apply full left rudder. The sun cascades through the canopy as the little yellow Slingsby departs over to the left of Jos`s shoulder. I am sat in the right-hand seat, and the aircraft turns tighter whilst I hold full pro spin inputs.

I am on an instructor's course, it is mid-January, and I have just had my fifty-ninth birthday. I am in good hands, as I have known Jos for a long time. He is a former RAF Red Arrow pilot from the 1980s, and is competent at what he does. He too has recently retired, from the same airline I had spent the majority of my career with, and I always came away from check rides that Jos had conducted feeling I had walked out with more than I had walked in with.

The instructor's course I am on is the result of recognising that I could not keep away from aircraft, and was inexorably drawn back to them. I renewed my licence, and having always stayed connected with light aircraft flying, was convinced by Graham Turner, the CFI at Goodwood aerodrome, that I should do it as it was "bloody good fun!" Plus, the opportunity to pass on knowledge accumulated over a lifetime appealed to me.

I had instructed briefly in my mid-twenties, and the Civil Aviation Authority (quite rightly) had concluded it was probably best if I did a full course as it was a very long time ago, part of which is the spin training. The most important part of the training is the 'recognition' of the conditions that can lead to a stall, so it is, in essence, spin prevention training.

As I reach the end of the second spin, I apply full opposite rudder and ease the stick slightly forward off the back stop, and the aircraft starts to slow its rotation . . . and flicks immediately into a spin to the right. Not what I expected. I now have spin recovery inputs (or what I think is spin recovery inputs) being applied and, in fact, have pro spin inputs in the new direction of rotation.

Jos sorts out the mess and we climb back up. The gyros have toppled on the instrument panel, and so have mine! He asks how I feel, and I admit to feeling queasy but certainly not to the point where I think there is any likelihood of being ill.

We climb back up and Jos surmises that I was slow with the recovery rudder input and the 'one second pause', as per the flight manual and briefing, was probably more like two or three before I moved the stick forward.

I enter another spin, this time to the right, and blow me if the same thing doesn't happen again, where in the recovery I flick the aircraft into a spin to the left.

By this time Jos has worked out what it is I am doing, or more correctly not doing, and demonstrates before I climb up and spin again. 'Muscle memory' is something we develop over time if we operate one particular aircraft or one particular car. The way you position yourself for a corner and the amount you turn the steering wheel is completely different in a high performance car to, say, an SUV, for example.

Aircraft are no different, and the spinning I had done thirty-five years earlier was always in basic trainers with thick chord wings, such as Cessna 150s and 152s where, as soon as you put in opposite rudder and released back pressure without much forward control input, the wings un-stall.

The Slingsby was different and Jos emphasised the need for positive firm inputs: bang, bang, bang. Full opposite rudder, bang, one second, briskly forward stick until the wings are un-stalled. Immediately rotation stops, centralise the rudders and 'ease' out of the dive. The important part was the forward stick input, and just how significantly more was required than what I was used to.

As I pull back up, having recovered from the spin I had just completed, I can feel the G just gently pushing me into my seat.

Lesson learnt.

Undoubtedly it is extremely important to have respect for the aircraft you fly and understand what it is that is required to keep you safe. All aircraft types have different characteristics and the lesson learnt was priceless: what worked on a Cessna did not work on a Slingsby, and that could prove fatal. In short: know your aircraft.

As I walked away from that bright yellow Slingsby, outside the hangars, I glanced back with gratitude, for in that one flight I had been reminded just how little I actually knew about flying, and how much more there is to learn. In aviation, the reality is we spend our entire careers as students, something we should never forget.

I am still learning . . .

References

Copyright and Permissions
The author attempted to contact all sources and obtain copyright permission. Whilst the vast majority readily gave the requisite permissions, some requests went unanswered and should at any stage permission be denied in the future all subsequent publications will be amended accordingly.

Chapter 2
London Gazette, 14th January 1916

Chapter 3
G-ARUD: ICAO Accident Digest No.14 Volume II, Circular 71-AN/63 (36-45)
https://aviation-safety.net/database/record.php?id=19620304-0

G-ASID: https://www.baaa-acro.com/operator/cale-

donian-airways
G-ARWE: ICAO Aircraft Accident Digest 18-II
https://aviation-safety.net/database/record.
php?id=19680408-0

Chapter 4
Mostert, N. *Supership* (SBN 333 17923 4), Macmillan London Ltd

Chapter 5
'Once in a Lifetime' by Talking Heads, produced and co-written by Brian Eno

Chapter 6
BBC News
http://news.bbc.co.uk/onthisday/hi/dates/stories/july/16/newsid_2503000/2503947.stm

Chapter 10
Alaska 261
https://www.ntsb.gov/investigations/AccidentReports/Reports/AAR0201.pdf

Chapter 11
N5934S
https://app.ntsb.gov/pdfgenerator/ReportGeneratorFile.ashx?EventID=20001213X32528&AKey=1&RType=Final&IType=FA

Jetstream 31
https://www.heraldscotland.com/news/12695211.
prestwick-air-crash-a-tragic-accident/

Hawker Hunter
https://assets.publishing.service.gov.uk/me-
dia/5422f5f0ed915d1374000589/dft_avsafety_
pdf_502233.pdf

Hawk Trainer
https://www.flightglobal.com/news/articles/dis-
connected-ailerons-are-blamed-for-raf-hawk-
crash-17706/
Reed Business Information Limited

Shoreham Mid-Air Collision
https://assets.publishing.service.gov.uk/me-
dia/5422ec3340f0b613460000e3/Vans_RV-
6A_G-RVGC_and_DA_40D_Diamond_Star_G-
CEZR_06-12.pdf

Andrews, J. W, 'Unalerted Air to Air Visual
Acquisition' (November 1991), Massachusetts
Institute of Technology

Chapter 14
https://www.youtube.com/watch?v=jWIFyH6M5mY
https://www.youtube.com/watch?v=lU0s_HL8khs

Chapter 17

Aerospace Medical Association http://www.asma.org/home
http://www.asams.org/guidelines/Completed/
NEW%20Retinal%20Detachment.htm